This rose is called *Touch of Class*. The blooms you see are what this book is all about—great modern roses.

How can you tell what makes a rose great? Start by looking at the bloom from two directions. In profile, it should have a high, pointed center rising above the rest of the petals. Looking down on the bloom, you want to see a clearly defined center, petals unfurling around it symmetrically. Ideally, there will be a pinpoint bull's eye in the center of the bloom. There are some other things to look for as well, but we'll take those up in Chapter 9. Roses like *Gold Medal* (below) and *Europeana* (opposite) will sometimes give you one bloom per stem, but they are loveliest when the blooms appear in clusters. You can decide which it will be. In Chapter 4 I'll tell you how to coax your rosebushes into blooming with the number of blossoms per stem that suit you best.

Rosarians dislike being asked to name their favorite rose because it means reducing a dozen or so irresistible beauties to only one variety. I beat around the bush for years, but finally settled on *Color Magic* (above). Its deep rose buds mature into huge, ravishing beige and pastel pink blossoms. Fragrance is delicious all the while. Can you blame me? Color Magic may not become your favorite, especially if you have an aversion to pink. Should you prefer red, yellow, white, even mauve, I'll tell you about good roses in those colors too.

Growing Good Roses

by Rayford Clayton Reddell

foreword by M. F. K. Fisher

photographs by the author

1817

HARPER & ROW, PUBLISHERS, *New York*

Cambridge, Philadelphia, San Francisco, Washington, London,
Mexico City, São Paulo, Singapore, Sydney

FIRST EDITION

A YOLLA BOLLY PRESS BOOK

Growing Good Roses was produced in association with the publisher at The Yolla Bolly Press, Covelo, California, under the supervision of James and Carolyn Robertson. Editorial and design staff: Barbara Youngblood, Diana Fairbanks, Renee Menge. Composition by Wilsted & Taylor, Oakland, California.

LIBRARY OF CONGRESS CATALOGING-IN-PUBLICATION DATA
Reddell, Rayford Clayton.
    Growing Good Roses.

    1. Rose culture—United States.   2. Roses—United States.   I. Title.
SB411.R39   1988   635.9'3372   87–12030
ISBN 0-06-055067-8

88 89 90 91 92   10 9 8 7 6 5 4 3 2 1

"God gave us memories
so we could have roses in winter
and mothers forever."

This book is dedicated to
the memory of
Saih Vidrine Reddell.

If you would like to grow the queen of flowers but can't decide what varieties to plant, this book will help you make up your mind. In Chapter 9 I will try to seduce you with my 24 sure-fire Best Bets. In Chapter 10 you'll read about some notorious roses that I consider greatly overrated (and some that I think are sleepers).

If you can't find just the right roses in this book, you should probably visit the nearest rose garden where you'll find others to choose from. The garden in Timaru, New Zealand (above), has one well-labeled rose variety planted in each bed. Rome's municipal rose garden (opposite) is landscaped around dramatic architecture. Many communities have public rose gardens. You'll find one close to home.

Roses dot the landscape in private gardens you can visit too. At Filoli (opposite), in Woodside, California, rose trees (called standards) rise above ground covers and complement other formal plantings. Standards are good solutions to the problem of crowding. You can squeeze in more roses even when it appears that you have run out of garden space.

Roses bloom in every color but blue. There are numerous blue ground covers and annuals to select if you want blue. A bed of delphinium (above) is accented because its color contrasts with everything else. In Chapter 4, I will try to persuade you not to plant anything under or right around your rosebushes. Instead, I will urge you to save room for a blanket of nutritional, handsome mulch.

This cutting plot (above) takes up a small corner of a much larger garden. Since the owner is primarily interested in roses for the house, the colors here aren't expected to harmonize with the rest of the garden because the blooms will be cut and brought indoors as quickly as they are ready. If you prefer to look at roses on their bushes rather than in vases, I'll suggest in Chapter 11 how to keep your garden from becoming a hodgepodge of color.

The garden at my San Francisco residence (opposite) has four narrow terraces because the lot slopes sharply. More than 100 rosebushes are squeezed into the small space by combining them with standards and miniatures. When 100 were no longer enough to satisfy me, I went commercial and now have a rose ranch with more than 4,000 bushes—barely enough.

Table of Contents

Shaping the Bush
What to Take/Leave
Where to Cut
At the Bud Union
After Pruning

Taking Exception to Ratings
Follies
Miniatures
Standards
Climbers

Roses in Containers
Landscaping with Roses
Companion Planting
Two New Ways of Growing
Your Own Rose

Foreword

Dear Ray:

". . . roses in winter and mothers forever."

I don't know who first said this quotation, which appears in your book, but I am fond of it (in a vaguely vain way) because I am a mother, just like Edith Kennedy (mine), Saih Reddell (yours), and Sidonie Colette. Sido, who was the mother of Colette, loved roses, but refused to grow them seriously—as they *must* be grown. She kept spindly clippings (as did Saih and Edith and even I), and she used to chuck them under their chins to lift up their faces, as if they were her children.

I think we are all in the same boat: we love roses, helplessly, stubbornly. If I could be one, I'd be full-blown, with a heart not so full-blown that there is nothing left but the petals. I'd be like my mother . . . like the first rose she ever spoke of to me: the Frau Karl Druschki—tall, pale, richly perfumed. . . .

Of course, I feel that almost every rose I see is the most perfect one I have ever seen. And I know people who grow roses for themselves, not to sell. They are what you, Ray, call rosarians. Then there are the real "growers," who may or may not sell their products.

You will always be a rosarian, even though you do grow them commercially. There is even publicity about you now and then! When I ask, "How did you find enough roses in your garden for this or that wedding (or the opening night of the opera, or ———, or ———)?" you say nonchalantly that there were fifteen thousand, or fifteen thousand dozen, or fifteen hundred dozen—whatever was needed—and that they happened to be ready to be flown across the country, or brought to a nearby church. You are cool about it, unperturbed. So I suppose I would say that a rosarian is a person who loves roses and who can grow them if he wishes to.

You must know about pruning and about things like aphids and mildew and all that, while Sido and the rest of us don't want to. We realize that raising roses is a learned art—and too much trouble! And we agree with you that the English have known most of our words much longer than we have here in America. So why *not* call a long stem with many blossoms on it a "cluster" and not a "grandiflora"?

And now to your own good English-American prose: I do admire the way you stay simple and correct. As you know, I didn't much want to read this book: Why bother about roses and growing them, I wondered. But I'm glad I did. I have new respect for both rose-growers and rosarians, and I am pleased that you dedicated it to people like me, who really don't like to grow roses, but who know why their children do.

The first rose I remember that my mother loved was what she called, in her inimitable Anglo-Dresden accent, a Frau Karl Druschki. Then I remember the Cecile Brunners, or, as she pronounced the name, Sessle Br-r-rooners, rolling the *r* in her slightly operatic German. They were lovely, tight, little curly things like pink shells, multi-petaled, of course. They grew on pergolas and trellises everywhere, and used to snag tall people's hair. They were wonderful on May Day for the baskets we hung on old ladies' doors.

When we first went to Whittier, in about 1911, the county roads were still bordered with the free roses that senators and mayors and chambers of commerce begged the few orange ranchers and farmers to plant. They said, "Plant, plant, *plant!* People will come out from Iowa and think this is an earthly paradise!" And the free donations grew almost frantically, and then died of neglect. By 1918, when we moved down Painter Avenue to the Ranch, there were still roses along the roads. It never occurred to any of the ranchers to spray, irrigate, clip, prune. They *grew* the tag end of them, so beautiful: the Frau Karl Druschki; the common, bright scarlet, lushly blooming Ragged-Robins. But best of all, in my first years, were the ones that grew over the abandoned outhouses in Whittier.

Whittier was built about a hundred years ago by a band of Quakers who proved their social standing, in one way or another at least, by whether they had one-holers or two- or three-holers in their backyard. When the flush toilet came along, somewhat before we arrived in 1911, instead of removing the latrines and covering up the good supply of night soil, the settlers simply pushed their outhouses over, filled in the holes, and planted Gold of Ophir roses they had brought from Pennsylvania. The vines thrived on the unexpected bounty of the richness beneath them, and I remember great heaps of them in every backyard in Whittier, blazing like moons on fire, yellow, gold, pink—and in the shade. I'll always remember their lovely color.

There were other roses, of course, and there have been many since then. And Edith and Saih and Sido and I do thank you, Ray, for writing about them as you do. I sign myself, as always, and for us all.

M. F. K. Fisher
Glen Ellen, California

CHAPTER I
Preliminaries

Confessions of a Rose-struck Gardener

I remember the first rose I saw.

I was a small boy, following my mother up the steps to a relative's house. There beside the walkway were two yellow rosebushes in full bloom. I stopped in my tracks, astonished by their beauty. I can still see those roses, yellow as butter in the Louisiana sunlight.

I asked my mother why we didn't have any roses. "They're too much trouble," she said. Mother had a way of sounding pretty final, and I put roses out of my mind.

In 1970 I bought a Victorian house in San Francisco, a building so run-down that it had been condemned. With the house came a backyard: a sloping sand dune that had never been cultivated. The restoration went slowly, so I began to garden in order to escape the plaster and sheetrock dust. The vegetables I planted did tolerably well, but didn't inspire me, and I lost interest in gardening after two years.

Then one night I had dinner with a friend who lived on Nob Hill. Pat Martin was not only a fabulous cook—she used to plan whole meals around the homemade sausage my father sends me from Louisiana. She was also a gifted gardener. On this particular evening, she served a dessert garnished with chocolate formed on Savoy cabbage leaves. It was a memorable finish to a perfect meal, but the "cabbages" I remember even more vividly were the roses she had set out everywhere in bud vases. The blooms were huge—the kind you want to touch to see if they're real.

Pat knew about my lackluster efforts to grow vegetables. She also knew that I was just then trying to give up cigarettes and needed both an outlet for my nervous energy and something to do with my hands. She practically ordered me to grow roses. "They're a lot of work," she said, sounding at that moment a lot like my mother, "and an enormous pleasure."

The starter set Pat gave me comprised the twelve varieties she liked best (I still have nine of the original bushes). I planted them in my backyard sand dune, after I had considerably enriched it with peat moss and fertilizer. The results were not spectacular. Some of the bushes did bloom, but since I had elected not to spray, mildew had wrought such havoc by midsummer that I had to completely defoliate more than one bush and start over.

The next year I joined the San Francisco chapter of the American Rose Society. And I sprayed. For the first time my neighbors began to refer to my backyard as a rose garden. I began going to rose shows and saw varieties that I wanted to grow. I learned to appreciate form, balance, and proportion as well as color, scent, and stem length. The more I learned about roses, the more my addiction grew. I increased my bushes to one hundred. The first rose I entered in a competition, a bloom of the Chinese lacquer red rose Olé, won a blue ribbon. Then I won the Novice Sweepstakes in both the San Francisco Rose Show in May and the San Francisco Flower Show in August. I was hooked.

Over the next several years, I thought constantly about how to find room for more and more bushes. I planted them in containers on my sundeck, in my too-shady front yard, in precarious spots near side fences. In the end, although I had almost to inch through the garden sideways, I got nearly two hundred bushes in my 25-foot-by-40-foot backyard. When I couldn't possibly squeeze in one more bush, the next step was inevitable.

I went commercial. I had been selling blooms at a flower shop near the house for quite a while and had found that there was an eager market for the large, long-lived, fragrant garden roses my backyard was producing. Still, friends tried to talk me out of a commercial venture. "Selling blooms from your garden is one thing," they said, shaking their heads, "but growing outdoor roses as a business is much too risky a proposition."

But there was no use talking to me. I was incurably rose-struck, and I would have my rose farm, risky or not.

When I saw Garden Valley Ranch, I knew my idea would work. It is in Petaluma, a rural market town forty-three miles north of San Francisco. The land I fell in love with is a meadow beside a working dairy. To the west are gentle hills that roll toward the sea. The site had the cool, foggy nights I was used to in the city, a climate roses adore if you control mildew. The soil is sandy and easily mixed, and water is ample. It rarely gets to 100 degrees in summer and seldom freezes in winter.

With the help of some less-skeptical friends, we planted 1,200 bushes in December 1980. Although a few problems arose—the wind, the thrips, the voracious cucumber beetles, the infernal gophers—the success of Garden Valley Ranch has exceeded our rosiest expectations. We now have more than 4,000 bushes in hundreds of varieties, and sell about 90 percent of our blossoms. We ship blooms across the country and have proved that garden roses have a market. We also practice every single suggestion in this book.

I have stopped competing, although I still could (the American Rose Society allows commercial-grower members to compete as long as their entries are taken from their private gardens). Now I am interested in hybridizing and exploring innovative growing practices.

Looking over the chapter headings in this book makes me cringe as I remember my mistakes. I made almost every one I will warn you about. I fell for misleading catalogue descriptions and ordered roses that proved to be flops. I planted bushes too deep and didn't fertilize them at all the first year because someone at a nursery said I shouldn't. My idea of maintaining bushes was to water them a lot when sunny weather made me want to be outside, and practically not at all when it was dreary. At first, I didn't spray, period; when I did, I launched a random, totally ineffective program. I cut every bloom with as much stem as I wanted, in casual disregard for the need to shape bushes. Pruning to me meant removing only what was visibly dead.

One thing is certain: mother was right. Roses are a lot of trouble. But they sure do make up for it. When I get home in the evening, I change into jeans, get my shears, and head out back to the garden. Once I start, it's hard to stop. There's always something to do. Perhaps a new variety is blooming for the first time, and I have to decide if it's anything like what I was hoping for. Or new growth appears in a strategic place, and I want to train it in the right direction with some early staking. And then there's the delicious agony of what to cut, and for whom.

My purpose in writing this book is simple. If you already grow roses well, I want you to grow them better. If you don't grow them well, I want to improve your chances for success. If you don't grow them at all, I want to encourage you to start.

Rose Classifications

While this book is all about roses, it's not about all of them. Today there are forty-eight official classifications of roses in commerce in the United States, including ancient varieties. I don't profess to be an expert on all of them, but I do understand those called modern, more particularly *hybrid teas*, *floribundas*, and *grandifloras*. These three types of modern roses, plus *miniatures* and *climbers*, which we'll also consider, make up more than 90 percent of the rosebushes sold in America. These are the roses with which we'll deal in this book.

When did roses become modern? All but the most ornery of rosarians agree that it was with the introduction of La France by Guillot Fils in 1867. This rose, the prototype of what we now call the hybrid tea, was just what the nineteenth-century rose breeders were looking for—a large, double (sixty petals) flower with a long, pointed bud. But the real find was La France's enviable habit of producing blooms with the fabulous form that we now call classic formal. It was a welcome shot in the arm for developers of new rose varieties, who scrambled to include pollen from La France on their hybridizing palettes.

Modern roses are so different from those now called old that it's impossible to lump the two together. Some older varieties flower only once per season, while most modern rosebushes bloom repeatedly. Growth habits differ too, with modern rosebushes being more bush-like than the shrubby older ones. Mostly, though, it's in the form of the blossoms that they are so different—older roses are essentially more decorative. Less importance is placed on the form of individual blooms. With the modern varieties the form of the bloom is vital.

Before you can be expected to appreciate varying forms, you must learn the basic differences between the three types of modern roses we'll be talking about. While there are several ways of distinguishing between hybrid teas, floribundas, and grandifloras, the easiest pertains to blossoms and blooming characteristics.

Hybrid Teas

These are the classic one-to-a-stem roses. Hybrid teas are capable of producing clustered blooms—and will if you don't follow the disbudding (bud removal) procedures described later—but aesthetic perfection for this variety is one bloom per stem. And should you care to exhibit your roses, hybrid teas must almost always be shown this way.

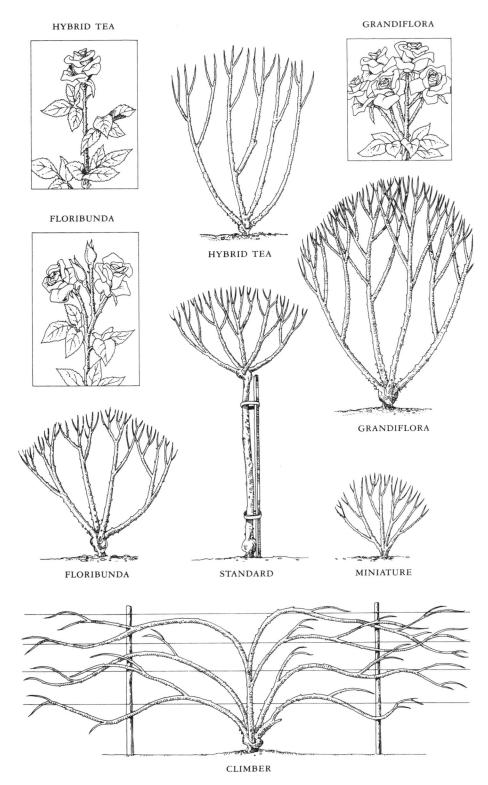

HYBRID TEA

FLORIBUNDA

HYBRID TEA

GRANDIFLORA

GRANDIFLORA

FLORIBUNDA

STANDARD

MINIATURE

CLIMBER

GROWTH AND BLOOM FORMS

Hybrid teas *are bred to produce one showy rose per stem.* **Floribundas** *are low-growing bushes that bloom in sprays of small, usually decorative, blossoms.* **Grandifloras** *are similar to floribundas, with sprays of blooms, but their blossoms are formed like hybrid teas.* **Miniature** *roses are diminutive versions of other rose forms. Minis grow on their own roots, so they have no bud unions.* **Climbers** *are distinguished by the way their bushes grow; they're hybridized to sprawl, but must be trained to ramble where you want them.* **Standards** *, or tree roses, are bushes that bloom atop a length of rosewood that has no growth along its sides.*

The "hybrid" portion of the name refers to hybridizers' efforts to mix rose lineage and come up with something new. "Tea" refers to the fact that they are descended from the tea rose, which originated in China. Also, the fragrance of hybrid teas is thought to be similar to that of fresh tea leaves.

Floribundas

These are roses hybridized to grow in clusters. The disbudding tactic is the opposite of that for the hybrid tea, as it is aimed at producing multiple blooms at the end of one stem. Though there are great exceptions, floribunda bushes are usually low in stature, making them perfect for foreground planting.

Grandifloras

These are the newest roses on the scene. Continued hybridizing of the floribunda resulted in seedlings that had the blooming characteristics of the floribunda (with multiple blooms on one stem), but whose blossoms were formed more like those of the hybrid tea. Hence, the new category of grandiflora. Though some are low, most grandifloras tend to be tall growers and to make majestic background plantings.

Classification of roses in the United Kingdom is far more sensible than it is in the United States. Recognizing the inevitable danger of confusion with the floribunda, the British never adopted a grandiflora class. They've even dropped the use of hybrid tea and floribunda classifications for rose exhibition. Instead, they refer to either "large-flowered" or "clustered-flowered" blooms. There are sound reasons behind the English classification. Americans, however, must still deal with the three categories just described and do their best to understand the differences among them. It's not always easy.

For instance, it's downright confusing when varieties of one classification grow so disparately. If you see bushes of Angel Face and Sea Pearl growing next to one another, you'll wonder how they both could possibly belong to the floribunda class. On the one hand, Angel Face grows very low, virtually hugging the ground. Sea Pearl, on the other hand, has lofty aspirations and won't stay down.

Rather than expecting varieties of a given classification to perform like their siblings, you will need to learn to consider each variety on its own, allowing also for regional variations that can markedly affect growth habits. Roses can climb, sprawl, hide the ground, grow erect, be trained as a pillar, or cover a wall. Bushes may be small, midsize, or enormous, depending on their natural habits, how they're pruned, and the care they're given. They all, however, possess anatomical similarities with which you might want to familiarize yourself.

Can You Grow Roses?

If you follow only most of the advice in this book, you will certainly be able to grow the queen of flowers. If you follow all of my suggestions, you'll have exhibition-quality blooms by the score, assuming, of course, that you can provide the right conditions.

As you'll learn in Chapter 3, roses have some basic requirements. You can get around some; others are impossible to circumvent. For instance, water. If you haven't a ready water supply or if you won't use what you have, don't plant roses, for they're insatiable drinkers. If you get little or no sun in your garden, roses probably aren't for you either, although I've seen people manage to produce sensational roses with what must surely be minimum direct sunlight.

If you have inherited rosebushes without knowing their history, the first thing you should do is find out what varieties they are. Plan to get rid of whatever you don't like and to coddle those you want to keep.

Most modern rosebushes come with a metal I.D. somewhere near their bud union. Look for it. If the tag has been exposed to the elements for a long time, the paint may have weathered off. Even so, you can usually feel the letters, since most are stamped into the metallic disk. If there's no identification whatsoever, wait until the bush is in bloom; then either look it up in a book or, better yet, ask an American Rose Society consulting rosarian to have a look.

Don't make the mistake of keeping varieties that you don't like; it makes no sense to give rosebushes the care they deserve if you aren't swept away by their blooms. After all, the least expensive part of growing roses is buying plants; bushes cost far less than the nutrients and spray materials they require, to say nothing of your valuable time while ministering to them.

Start taking good care of whatever you keep, applying the tips from Chapter 4, especially those on fertilizing. Regardless of when they were last fed, it's safe to assume that roses are hungry. They'll be thirsty too.

Drastic measures might be necessary at pruning time, just to correct mistakes that someone else made. Neglected rosebushes have gnarled, grayish brown wood that you should hack out without a second thought. Even if you have to lop off half the bush, get rid of wood that's past producing. Bushes that are too tall should be shortened and thinned; those that have been pruned too enthusiastically should be left alone to reach heights where they'll bloom comfortably. Local rosarians will advise what to do to which, but start by taking Chapter 8 to heart.

You just may have inherited some old roses in addition to modern varieties. I did. When I bought the property where I grow roses commercially, some dilapidated Victorian buildings came with it. The first time I looked at the old farmhouse, I noticed a huge rosebush on its west side. At first, I thought it was a hedge, but when I got closer I realized it was just one overgrown shrub. Even though I had no idea what variety it was, I made a mental note to take it out and replace it with something more civilized.

When pruning time rolled around and I stripped the bush to get a better look at it, I realized that I had better leave it just where it was since it camouflaged drainage and water pipes, and, more recently, propane flex-lines. I shaped the bush and left it alone. I've since learned that it's *Rosa laevigata*, better known as the Cherokee Rose—Georgia's state flower. It has five-petaled, white flowers and apple green foliage, and it is a sight to behold every May and early June.

Old rose varieties make their contribution to the garden, mostly in landscaping. I'd never give up my modern roses for them because I need a succession of blossoms from spring through fall. Most old garden roses have only one bloom—early, abundant, and spectacular—after which they're occasional repeaters.

If you are ready to add roses to your garden, I'll suggest varieties to suit your particular landscape, tell you about growing roses in containers (a nice solution for those with limited space), suggest how to crowd in more rosebushes when you seem to have run out of space, mention the advantages of mixing varieties or sticking with one or two, and make some general comments about probable size and height of bushes, though you'll learn that where you live makes a huge difference.

If you are an aspiring rosarian and have not yet established bad habits, you are the ideal reader of this book. You can buy, plant, and maintain roses properly from the start. If you already grow roses, but aren't satisfied with them or their yield, you will find that it's not too late to adjust techniques. If nothing more, concentrate on the chapter on cutting and at least get extended life from the blooms you're already producing. Or if your bushes are disease ridden by midsummer every year, you might give in to trying chemical sprays, using the safe but effective spraying methods I suggest. If you're never going to be satisfied with the roses you have because they're the wrong varieties, it might be wise to replace some of them with surefire winners I propose in Chapter 9.

Everyone has *some* place for a rose. If nothing else, there can be a potted miniature on a window ledge, though I'm going to try to talk you into *much* more.

CHAPTER 2
Buying

You may as well begin with the right roses if you mean to give them the care they deserve and to reap for yourself the many pleasures of successful rose culture. What you buy depends on where you live, how much space you have, whether you plan to exhibit, and, of course, on what you like.

In Chapter 9 I suggest some great modern roses you should consider. Hybrid teas, floribundas, and grandifloras are included. It's true that most are hybrid teas, but that's because varieties of this type vastly outnumber the other two. Assuming that you can have more than one bush and that you don't already have a strong, preconceived preference, please treat yourself to all three. If one is your present limit, start with a hybrid tea.

Winners

Unless you're an ardent pioneer, go with proven performers. Besides those I suggest in Chapter 9, there are two good ways of identifying them. First, the American Rose Society (hereafter called simply ARS) identifies star performers in its annual publication *Handbook for Selecting Roses*.

Here's how the system works. First, roses are classified as to type—for our purposes, hybrid tea, floribunda, or grandiflora. Next, there is color classification with seventeen categories, including blends and shadings of major colors. Finally, there is the national rating, representing the collective opinions of voting rosarians from all districts in the United States. Now, we know that certain varieties do better or poorer in various sections of the country, but those regional differences have a way of evening out in the final analysis, generally making the average score a safe one.

Each year the voting ARS members rank new introductions and thereafter reconsider merit with periodic reviews called "proof of the pudding." The final results, a numerical assignment on a scale of 1.0

to 10.0 for each variety, are published annually in the *Handbook for Selecting Roses*. The one score represents an average of values for garden bloom performance and for exhibition value. The national scoring ratings are:

10.0	Perfect
9.9–9.0	Outstanding
8.9–8.0	Excellent
7.9–7.0	Good
6.9–6.0	Fair
5.9 and lower	Of questionable value

The *Handbook* can be had by sending one dollar and a self-addressed, stamped envelope to American Rose Society, Box 30000, Shreveport, Louisiana 71130.

The second way to discover which roses to grow is to join the ARS and your local ARS chapter. If you are even casually interested in roses, I strongly suggest that you consider doing so.

The first rose show I attended, right after I got seriously addicted to roses, was sponsored by the San Francisco Rose Society, which had a booth where information was being distributed to those interested enough to ask. I wasn't sure what I wanted to know, but I talked with the woman there. Her first suggestion was that I join the San Francisco chapter of the ARS. Her second and even more valuable tip was to buy a copy of *Growing Roses in San Francisco*, a 120-page booklet published by the San Francisco Rose Society. The five dollars it cost me has proven to be the best single investment in roses I've ever made.

There is no substitute for getting a handle on what happens in your immediate area, and no easier way to find out than through the ARS. Anyone, member or not, can write to the society and ask for the names of consulting rosarians in his or her area. The roster is free. Long before you run out of questions to ask the listed expert(s), you'll probably be eager to join the local society. Even if you don't want to join, you are perfectly welcome at monthly meetings and will be cordially treated to a lot of interesting information.

Other advantages of ARS membership include receiving regional publications; a national monthly magazine, which occasionally has helpful articles and always contains commercial information; and a yearly *Rose Annual*, which includes truly useful articles and the very latest information.

If you decide to contact your locally appointed rosarians, have some specific questions in mind. You might be after strong rose fragrance, specific colors, high bloom yield, varieties with few thorns, blooms that close at night, or long-lasting cut blossoms. Seeking local advice will help you avoid varieties that do poorly in your region. After this initial call, don't throw away the telephone number; you're sure to want to use it again.

Consulting rosarians are the very same people you should contact if you inherit some established rosebushes. It would be helpful to know what they are, in order to give them optimum care or to learn if they're worth keeping at all.

Don't hesitate to call; your inquiries will be more welcome than you might imagine. Often when I'm asked this favor, people spend most of the conversation apologizing for requesting my time when, they say, they know I have so many "better" things to do. Truth is, I love it, for what else can one do with this storehouse of rose trivia?

By the way, it would be helpful to call when there are some flowers on the bush. The best of us have real trouble when there are no blooms for clues.

Nurseries

Thank goodness for the local nurseries. They're indispensable when you suddenly discover that you have some insect you're not equipped to spray for, when your roll of expandable tape runs out and you have a huge branch to tie up, or when a bush needs a particular kind of food that you don't have on hand. I frequent nurseries for all these reasons and more, but I don't buy my roses from them. First, nurseries rarely stock bareroot bushes, and I prefer avoiding all containers. Moreover, the selection isn't wide enough. Nurseries tend to deal with only one supplier, usually a grower who limits varieties to those his staff has hybridized. You might get something wonderful, but chances are you will miss out on some great roses if you depend on a single source.

Bareroot or in a Container?

I bought no bareroot bushes the first year I grew roses. I started too late in the season to buy them, and I had an uneasy feeling about them besides. Handling fistfuls of sticks just didn't feel comfortable, and I wasn't optimistic that they'd amount to much. I got over my worries, and so will you when you come to appreciate the advantages of bareroot plants. First, aiming at your practical side, they're cheaper. Bushes in containers cost more than bareroot plants, not just because of the containers themselves, but because of the labor required to put the bushes in them. Also, roots must be compressed to fit within container constraints. Finally, container roses have to readjust to the soil in their new home after they are either removed from their cans or grow through their biodegradable containers. Bareroots, however, can be planted exactly as you want them to grow, as you'll learn in the next chapter.

Rose Suppliers and Their Catalogues

I hesitate to recommend a bareroot supplier with whom I've not personally dealt, so my list of American nurseries is limited to the four from which I have purchased. They are Jackson & Perkins, Box 1028, Medford, Oregon 97501; Roses by Fred Edmunds, 6235 S.W. Kahle Road, Wilsonville, Oregon 97070; Spring Hill Nurseries, Box 1714, Peoria, Illinois 61656; and Stocking Rose Nursery, 785 N. Capitol Avenue, San Jose, California 95133.

Suppliers such as these have lots to recommend them—they have wide selections of rose varieties and efficient shipping methods that assure healthy plants, timely in their arrival. If shipment is unduly delayed or stock is beneath your expectations, most suppliers will replace plants with no questions asked.

Catalogues can be misleading. They sometimes suggest that certain varieties have highly desirable qualities (powerful fragrance, extreme vigor, disease-resistance, bountiful bloom), which, if you grow them, you're apt to find they don't have at all. Color photos can make a variety look better than it looks in real life or lend a hue to which it can never truly aspire. Others are pitifully unjust and either rob the poorly depicted variety of its true color or fail to capture its exquisite form. Order catalogues anyway. They're free, and you can compare them for varieties on which suppliers agree. Above all, learn catalogue lingo. "Tender" means the variety is likely to freeze. "Disease-prone" suggests rampant mildew. "Powerfully fragrant" describes roses from which you can safely count on scent. "Light fragrance" may very well mean no discernible aroma.

Visit your closest municipal rose garden. There you can see numerous varieties and decide for yourself which appeal to you and which obviously perform well. Also, you can usually preview new introductions not yet rated by the ARS.

One catalogue I believe you should have will cost you two dollars.

Roses of Yesterday and Today on Brown's Valley Road in Watsonville, California 95076, specializes in old roses, though they carry some modern ones too. Varietal descriptions are accurate and charming. When I first grew roses and didn't yet know of this wonderful supplier, a woman I met, who grew not a single rose, lent me her copy. After a week, when I was still reading it with delight and calculating how many varieties I could squeeze into my yard the next year, my friend called me. She wondered if I might return her catalogue soon, confessing that, although she wasn't actually doing any planting, she missed it, since she read it from cover to cover at least once a week.

If you live in the United States, you are permitted to import plants directly from Canada with no restrictions. Importing from Europe is quite another matter. Permits are necessary, and you will be required to plant any imported bushes at least twenty feet, farther in some areas, from anything else. Representatives of government agencies responsible for this area of agriculture must visit you yearly and attest to your compliance. Don't even consider such a hassle for anything you can buy within the United States or Canada. For some few rare varieties, you may decide it's worth the trouble.

As long as Canadian bushes are allowed into this country without quarantine restrictions, let me give you one final recommendation. There is a perfectly wonderful rose nursery in Pickering, Ontario. Before writing to Pickering, though, you should know some things.

First, only a fraction of the available varieties are pictured in the catalogue, so you need to know exactly what you want to order. Second, the bushes are shipped during two periods. If you live in a temperate climate, you may have rosebushes for fall planting from late October through November. Otherwise, shipments for spring planting are made in March and April. Third, bushes bear little resemblance to those grown in Wasco, California, where the majority of bareroot bushes sold in the United States originate. Canadian bushes are diminutive compared to their American cousins. When I received the first plants I ordered from Pickering, I questioned the soundness of my choice of suppliers. They were tiny, not half the size of those from Wasco. They had, however, vastly more developed root systems. While I was dubious at planting time, all doubts were long gone by the end of the first growing season. The Canadian bushes became as large as any from American suppliers. I'm convinced that their complex root structure, including masses of hairlike roots, is the reason.

Finally, prices are cheaper than those here, but Pickering will send to the United States only roses whose patents have expired. The nursery adheres to this regulation in recognition of royalties due American hybridizers. So don't ask for any new varieties, even if they're offered for sale to Canadians. There are, however, numerous worthy nonpatented varieties, as you'll learn in Chapter 9.

To receive its list of available roses, including a large selection of old varieties, write to Pickering Nurseries, 670 Kingston Road, Pickering, Ontario L1V 1A6.

A devoted rosarian specializing in rose-plant availability can tell you where to find obscure varieties. Beverly Dobson annually compiles an exhaustive list of rose varieties, with a coding system telling where they can be bought. Her lists are invaluable, for they include European sources and instructions on how to obtain importing privileges. Her *Combined Rose List* can be obtained by writing to Beverly R. Dobson, 215 Harriman Road, Irvington, New York 10533.

Grading

Bushes being marketed by growers and suppliers must be graded according to specific standards. For the most part, you shouldn't consider any grade but 1. For hybrid teas and grandifloras, this means that bushes, after having been field grown for two years, must have at least three vigorous canes (main stems), each of a specific length. Floribundas are required to have the same number of canes, but they can be shorter. Grade 1½ denotes fewer canes, but may be acceptable if no grade 1's are available. Never buy grade 2. Most suppliers sell only grade 1 to the general public, so you'll never have to make the choice between 1 and 1½ unless you are notified that only grade 1½ is available, at a lower cost.

As for those wax-coated, packaged rose plants available in supermarkets, I can't honestly tell you never to buy them, but I'm tempted to. First, one rarely receives a guarantee as to variety or replacement (such assurances are routine from suppliers). More important, the waxing, while theoretically a sound procedure that permits prolonged and safe storage, is actually problem-ridden. Plants that are wax coated tend to dry out, and later growth and root development can be inhibited. Finally, the sun is supposed to melt the wax, but you may very well be planting long before heat from sunlight is going to be anywhere near intense enough to melt wax.

All-America Rose Selections

Each year since 1940 (except for 1951, when nothing seemed worthy) the AARS (All-America Rose Selections) has granted its ultimate award to one or several roses by declaring them the All-America Rose Selection for the following year. The selection is, of course, of great importance to a variety's likelihood for popularity. Hybrid teas, grandifloras, and floribundas are all candidates. For the most part, this designation is to be heeded; the majority of the roses I'm suggesting for you in Chapter 9 are also All-America Rose Selections. But for one reason or another, some real duds have earned this title; we'll talk about several of them. For the record, a list of the winners chosen since the award began appears on the opposite page.

All-America Rose Selections need not originate within the United States. Rose varieties from anywhere are eligible if an American supplier decides to introduce and subject them to the whims of the AARS standards committee. More than one-third of the roses listed as "Best Bets" in Chapter 9 are from abroad. The rest are American, though that has no bearing whatsoever on my choosing them.

"Roses of the Year"

Some growers annually declare a "Rose of the Year" award on their own. Be wary of them. Often such "winners" are being pushed on you because the grower invested heavily in planting the variety while it was under consideration for All-America Rose Selection and got caught with a surplus when it lost.

In defense of the growers, I must admit that sometimes their selections do pan out. When the great American hybridizer Bill Warriner came up with Pristine and had it available for introduction in 1978, Jackson & Perkins, for whom Warriner works, knew they had a real winner on their hands. They could have endured the two-year test period imposed by the All-America Rose Selection committee with confidence that Pristine would emerge a winner, but why? Instead, they named it their rose of that year and hoped the buying public would endorse their decision. It did. Pristine now enjoys the number-two spot on the list of top exhibition roses in the United States.

All-America Rose Selections are hardly the last word for identify-

ALL-AMERICA ROSE SELECTIONS

1940
Dicksons Red
Flash
The Chief
World's Fair

1941
Apricot Queen
California
Charlotte Armstrong

1942
Heart's Desire

1943
Grande Duchesse Charlotte
Mary Margaret McBride

1944
Fred Edmunds
Katherine T. Marshall
Lowell Thomas
Mme. Chiang Kai-shek
Mme. Marie Curie

1945
Floradora
Horace McFarland
Mirandy

1946
Peace

1947
Rubaiyat

1948
Diamond Jubilee
High Noon
Nocturne
Pinkie
San Fernando
Taffeta

1949
Forty-niner
Tallyho

1950
Capistrano
Fashion
Sutter's Gold
Mission Bells

1951
No selection

1952
Fred Howard
Helen Traubel
Vogue

1953
Chrysler Imperial
Ma Perkins

1954
Lilibet
Mojave

1955
Jiminy Cricket
Queen Elizabeth
Tiffany

1956
Circus

1957
Golden Showers
White Bouquet

1958
Fusilier
Gold Cup
White Knight

1959
Ivory Fashion
Starfire

1960
Fire King
Garden Party
Sarabande

1961
Duet
Pink Parfait

1962
Christian Dior
Golden Slippers
John S. Armstrong
King's Ransom

1963
Royal Highness
Tropicana

1964
Granada
Saratoga

1965
Camelot
Mister Lincoln

1966
American Heritage
Apricot Nectar
Matterhorn

1967
Bewitched
Gay Princess
Lucky Lady
Roman Holiday

1968
Europeana
Miss All-American Beauty
Scarlet Knight

1969
Angel Face
Comanche
Gene Boerner
Pascali

1970
First Prize

1971
Aquarius
Command Performance
Redgold

1972
Apollo
Portrait

1973
Electron
Gypsy
Medallion

1974
Bahia
Bon Bon
Perfume Delight

1975
Arizona
Oregold
Rose Parade

1976
America
Cathedral
Seashell
Yankee Doodle

1977
Double Delight
First Edition
Prominent

1978
Charisma
Color Magic

1979
Friendship
Paradise
Sundowner

1980
Love
Honor
Cherish

1981
Bing Crosby
Marina
White Lightnin'

1982
Brandy
French Lace
Mon Cheri
Shreveport

1983
Sun Flare
Sweet Surrender

1984
Impatient
Intrique
Olympiad

1985
Showbiz

1986
Broadway
Touch of Class
Voo Doo

1987
Bonica
New Year
Sheer Bliss

1988
Amber Queen
Mikado
Prima Donna

ing great varieties, but they're the best guide we have short of testing everything ourselves. So learn the difference between them and "roses of the year"—titles growers pragmatically confer themselves. All-America Roses have emerged triumphant from test gardens authorized by All-America Rose Selections Incorporated.

When to Order

When you place an order for bareroot rosebushes, you get to choose the delivery date. It can be ASAP or at the tag end of the shipping season, depending on when you think you'll feel like planting and when it's safe to do so where you live.

There's a move afoot among rosarians for fall planting, based on the theory that roots put in the ground in November have a chance to settle in before they have to start growing in the spring. I march with this group, but I can afford to because my winters are never severe enough to damage new, tender growth that's bound to appear soon after I stick a bush in the ground. If I lived where temperatures plummet regularly, I'd ask for rosebushes to be shipped after dangers of hard frosts are past.

Regardless of when you want plants to arrive, order them early to make sure you don't end up with substitutions, especially if a variety you like is "in short supply" or a catalogue specifies "one per customer, please." If you dilly dally, you'll get your money refunded or you'll be placed on next year's waiting list.

After you order whichever roses you decide on, dig holes at designated sites and prepare to do some planting. If you want to begin pampering your roses, dig planting sites early and give soil additives a chance to mellow.

CHAPTER 3
Planting

I wish I had met the man who said, "I'd rather plant a two-bit rose in a four-bit hole than a four-bit rose in a two-bit hole." He was a smart cookie: no matter what the quality of a rosebush, it can only live up to the hole in which it's planted. But before you dig and prepare the almighty hole, choose the site carefully.

Basic Site Requirements

Roses must have sun. According to most experts, the minimum is five hours per day. If the climate is temperate, full sunlight is preferable. In areas of intense heat, shading will be necessary, as roses suffer from temperatures over 100 degrees F. If you must choose between morning or afternoon sun, go for morning sun with shade in the afternoon.

Look for shelter from the wind; it damages both blooms and foliage. Plant near, but not against, fences and garden walls.

Don't plant roses near trees or large bushes where they will have to compete with other root systems. Rosebushes are voracious feeders and don't like sharing their nutrients with neighbors.

Since roses are always thirsty, choose growing sites in reasonable proximity to water sources.

Drainage is just as important as water. Although rose roots require steady amounts of water, they don't like to sit in it. Root damage occurs when water can't drain quickly and thoroughly. An easy way to determine if drainage is adequate is to fill a hole with water and see how long it takes to drain. If more than an hour is required, drainage must be improved by digging holes six inches deeper than you otherwise might have and filling them with six inches of coarse gravel.

The more claylike your soil is, the more concerned you must be with creating good drainage. Sandy soils drain well inherently. In fact, they may even require additives such as peat moss to provide water *retention*.

Space planting holes far enough apart to allow for both bush and root growth. I plant all hybrid teas and grandifloras three feet apart. Floribundas known to be diminutive in their growth habits can be planted closer together, as can any variety with which you want to create an impenetrable hedge (cheaper than most fences).

Getting the Bush Ready

If you plant bareroot bushes soon after you get them home from a reliable nursery or shortly after you receive them from a shipper, they will be in good condition. If planting has been delayed because of bad weather, bushes may have dried out. Moisture can be replenished if you submerge the bushes in water, covering all roots. Depending on how dried out the bushes have become, they can be soaked for up to twenty-four hours. After this treatment, the dried parts will plump and fill out nicely.

Some rosarians soak their rosebushes for two hours before they plant them no matter how quickly they arrived from the supplier. "Who knows how long ago they were dug up and left in cold storage?" they ask. These same clever gardeners suggest that you add some household bleach to your soaking tub, thereby cleaning up whatever unwanted bacteria might be hanging around. They'll also mention that a shot of all-purpose liquid fertilizer or Vitamin B-1 wouldn't hurt either.

Next, all broken stems and roots must have their damaged sections cut out. Using sharp shears, make a clean cut into healthy growth a quarter inch from the break. Many people cut off one-quarter inch of all root tips, claiming that this will help to stimulate new growth. I think it makes sense. Whether or not you clip everything, at least cut out damaged areas—they are a haven for disease. If canes are damaged, they too must be cut. Take off as little as possible at this time. Wait until after new growth appears to cut off anything else.

The Almighty Hole

I don't like to think about the time and fertilizers I've wasted by digging holes that are too deep. As a novice, I was informed that holes had to be two feet deep and two feet wide. Two feet is too deep for rose roots, which don't often get longer than one foot. I understand the supposed advantage of nutrients deep in the ground that roots eventually grow into, making the bushes act as if they have hit paydirt. But even if nutrients are placed there, they will have leached out from watering by the time roots reach them. I compromise and dig holes eighteen inches deep and two feet wide. As you'll learn, I prefer to do most of my fertilizing above soil level anyway.

I've stuck to digging holes two feet wide, though, because I've seen the advantages. If you dig up a bush that you've planted some six months earlier, you'll find masses of tiny hairlike growth projecting from all the roots you stuck in the ground six months ago. These "feeder roots" are the real workers, supplying bushes with nutrients, and they're everywhere within a two-foot radius of the center of most bushes. To develop massively, feeder roots must grow in friable (easily crumbled) soil.

Examine the soil you get from digging a hole eighteen inches deep by two feet wide. If you know or have been told that it's decent garden soil, save it. If it's too compact or reveals that it lacks nutritional value by being all one pale color, get rid of it and use one of the commercially available products. Packaged soil, such as Supersoil, is just what you'd like your basic soil to be—a loose, friable medium that mixes easily with additives.

Where I grow roses, the soil is almost pure sand from an old riverbed. It has some nutritional and trace elements and willingly accepts additives. If you have anything resembling garden loam, you're even better off. In fact, unless you're dealing with clay or heavily compacted soil, you can probably use what you have as half of what you need to refill the hole. The remaining half, in equal portions, should come from:

1. Aged manure. Cow and steer manures are the most readily available. Chicken is better, and rabbit better yet, as they contain higher percentages of nitrogen. Whichever you use, aging is important because fresh manure burns new roots with the intense heat it throws off during its early decomposition. Aged manure is sold at most nurseries in soft plastic forty-pound bags. For each hole you fill, you'll need about twenty pounds, or 7½ gallons.

2. Organic materials. Here you have a choice of several wonderful sources. One is peat moss, although it will probably be more expen-

sive than anything else. Composts made from redwood shavings, fir bark, or other shredded woody sources are cheaper. Since any of the organics will do, either singly or in combination, for the 12½ gallons (1½ cubic feet) you'll need per hole, watch for local nursery sales.

Don't overlook local sources of compost. We buy compost from a nearby mushroom farm. The soil mushrooms grow in is good for only one crop. Afterwards, it's spent for mushrooms, but nutritional for roses because it's composed of all their favorite foods.

If you use peat moss, you should be aware that because it is compressed for packaging, it will unrelentingly shed water if used straight from the package. To take advantage of its absorbing qualities, break up the compressed material and put it to soak in a large container that will allow total submersion (I use trash cans the day of garbage pickup). Soaked in water for twenty-four hours and then squeezed, peat moss will perform properly from the start.

If you use an organic material made from a wood derivative, remember that it should be in compost form. Raw sawdust, while of the right texture, needs nitrogen to break down and will rob the bush of any available sources of it. You might also look for one of the wood products available to which nitrogen has already been added. These products will break down on their own without usurping nitrogen needed by the bush.

Mix well the soil you saved, aged manure, and one of the organic materials, using a wheelbarrow or other large container if available. (If not, mix the soil in the hole itself.) After combining materials, fill half the hole and water well.

The next step is to create a cone of mounded soil over which the bareroot bush will be placed. But, first, an anatomy lesson.

The Bud Union

Bushes of modern roses are really a grafted combination of two separate rose varieties. "Rootstock" is the part underground. It comes from older varieties known not for their blooms, which are usually insignificant, even ugly, but rather for their capacity for massive root development. To this rootstock a graft is made of the rose variety desired to grow above the ground: the hybrid. Where the graft of the two varieties is made, a globular bulbous landmark develops that forever bears testament to the marriage.

The bud union is the heart of the rosebush. It is from there that

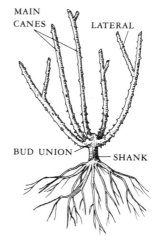

MAIN CANES   LATERAL

BUD UNION ———— SHANK

BAREROOT ROSEBUSH
Familiarize yourself with the parts of a bareroot rosebush. You must spot the bud union on sight to make sure you plant the bush to the right height. Learn also the difference between main canes and laterals.

major new growth will develop when conditions are right. Also, it is the point from which planting depth is measured. Assuming you mulch after planting, and I'm going to try very hard to persuade you to, the bud union can be placed above ground, level with the height to which you plan to mulch. Mulching materials will still cover the bud union sufficiently to protect it from freezing.

If, however, you live in an area where winters are hard and temperatures are extreme (below 20 degrees F.), you can't afford this luxury; for you proper planting usually requires the bud union to be at or below soil surface.

Forming a Cone

If you look at a bareroot rose plant, you'll see that although all the roots come from just beneath the bud union, they go their separate ways as soon as they leave and fan out their growth. If you consider that a bush should be planted to accommodate the way its roots seem to want to grow, it's hard to improve on a cone-shaped mound. With the bud union placed on top of the cone, roots can be draped over the broader base and spread out comfortably to rest.

How high the cone extends above ground level will be determined by bud union placement. If you follow my instructions for adding three to four inches of mulch after planting, the cone will have to rise above ground level by that amount. If hard freezes are a factor or if you refuse to mulch, the top of the cone will be at or just below soil surface.

A sturdy cone is best formed by gradually placing handfuls of the planting mixture and patting them down to eliminate large air pockets. Think of it as a tepee of soil rising out of the hole. Form it bit by bit. When at the right height, formed and compacted, it's ready to receive the bush. Check the right height for the bud union by laying a shovel handle or stick on the ground and across the hole.

Placing the Bush

With the cone mounded to the right height and the bush readied for planting, it's time for placement. Rose growers argue endlessly about which way the bud union should face. Since plants tend to grow toward the source of light, some claim that the lopsided portion of a new bush should be planted to the north. Others state that the bud union should face the greatest source of sun, no matter how this might affect the overall bush placement. I once experimented with placing bud unions of bushes of the same variety at every point I could within 360 degrees. I didn't detect one hoot of difference. Plant them facing the direction you like. If the bud union, with its tarred heart, bothers you, plant so you don't see it. If you like to see the bud union as a landmark against which to measure new growth, plant so you can see it.

Set the bush directly onto the tip of the cone, carefully spreading roots outward and downward. Then, holding the bush in place, begin filling in the rest of the hole, pressing down the soil mixture firmly enough to avoid air pockets, but being careful not to break any of the fragile roots. Use your hands, not your feet, to tamp down the soil. When half of the filling is completed, water to soak thoroughly and assemble the dry fertilizers while the hole is draining.

Dry Fertilizers

At planting time and once a year thereafter, bushes require dry fertilizers that break down gradually throughout the growing season. At all other times fertilizers are applied in liquid form so that nutrients are immediately available.

Commercial chemical fertilizers now have precise extended-release qualities which work wonderfully well. Marketing is by formulas expressed numerically for the basic elements: nitrogen, phosphorus, and potash. The three elements are *always* expressed in the same order—nitrogen first, then phosphorus and potash.

The best blend I've found is 18-6-12, formulated for a nine-month slow release. It really does work the way it's supposed to, and the release is triggered by soil temperature, so that the nutritional material won't go to work until growing conditions are right. The fertilizer is in the form of small granules about the size of coarse sand. You will need one-half cup per hole, distributed evenly around the base of the bush.

Several different organic fertilizers can be used, but I prefer hoof and horn (14-0-0) and bone meal (.5-30-0). Two cups of each one should be sprinkled right over the chemical fertilizers you just applied. I have used bone meal and fish meal as satisfactory substitutes for hoof and horn, and superphosphate instead of bone meal.

Dry fertilizers should be applied and watered into place before the remaining soil is added to fill the hole. Once water has drained, fill the hole and tamp down everything. Water again.

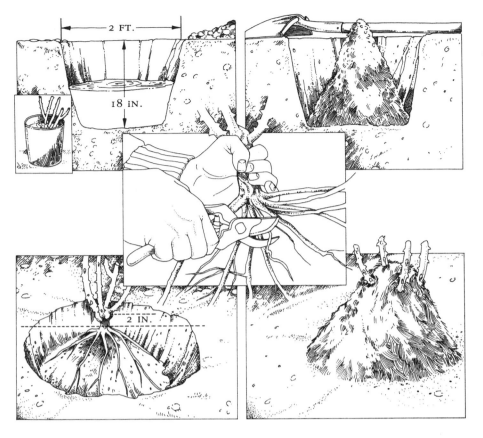

Mounding

I can't overemphasize the importance of this next step. Will you ever be sorry if you don't follow my advice! Unless newly planted bushes are mounded, all previous efforts will have been in vain. Bare-root rose canes left uncovered will dry out, and cold winter winds will parch them.

Any of the materials you've just been working with can be used for mounding; a combination of them would be ideal. Mix the left-over soil from the hole you dug with any of the suggested organic materials. Heap the combination over the bush until at *least* half of the plant is covered. Water it down, not away, and turn your back to the well-planted bush.

Containerized Bushes

Already-planted rosebushes come in two kinds of containers: rigid (metal or plastic) ones that must be removed or biodegradable ones that are planted intact. If you buy one in a metal container, have the

HOW TO PLANT A ROSE

Choose a site that gets shelter from the wind and at least five hours of sun each day. **Dig a hole** *two feet wide and eighteen inches deep and fill it with water. If it takes the hole more than an hour to drain, improve drainage by digging deeper and adding gravel.*

While you work on the almighty hole, **soak the bush** *in enough water to cover its roots. Add a little household bleach to the water to get rid of bacteria, and a liquid fertilizer to give the bush a head start.* **Form a cone** *by patting handfuls of planting mixture until you form a tepee of soil rising from the hole.*

Just before you put the bush in place, **trim off any damaged or broken roots** . *Use sharp shears to make a clean cut into the healthy growth a quarter inch from a break. Some rosarians cut off one-quarter inch of all root tips, claiming that it stimulates growth—probably a good practice.*

Place the bush *by draping its roots comfortably over the cone. Make sure the bud union is at the right height for the amount of mulch you plan to add. A shovel laid across the hole will help you gauge height.*

Holding the bush in place, begin to **refill** *the hole with soil that you pat down with your hands. When the hole is half filled, water to soak.* **Dry fertilizers** *should be sprinkled into the half-filled hole and watered into place before the rest of the soil is added.*

Mounding *is the final step for a well-planted bush. No matter which mounding materials you use, heap them to cover at least half the plant. Water again.*

nursery cut the container before you leave unless you have a can cutter at home. *Don't* pull the bush out of an uncut can; it will damage the roots.

If the soil around the roots is loose, try to get it all into the planting hole with as little disturbance as possible. If the soil is compressed into a ball of roots, rub and loosen it. You can't go so far as to spread out the roots, but you can make them more pliable and head them in the right direction.

Cones won't be necessary, but planting techniques for fertilizing, watering in, and soil compression are identical to those for bareroot plants, as is bud union placement.

Bushes in biodegradable containers are planted intact, but use the bud union, *not* the container lip, as the landmark for planting depth. If the bud union has sunk below the rim of the container, you will just have to live with the unsightly lip of the container until the biodegradable material disintegrates (usually within the first growing season). Since their leafy growth has already developed and shouldn't be covered, container bushes don't get mounded, but they should be planted with mulching in mind and with the bud union placed to the right height.

Once bareroot or containerized bushes are planted, they should be left alone. Keep them just on the wet side of moist. Nature may help you with periodic rainfalls. If not, water bushes and get ready to maintain them.

CHAPTER 4
Maintaining

With roses there's always something to do. Above all else, they must be watered. If you want more and bigger blooms, you must also fertilize. If certain flower formations are what you're after, you must watch for them as they form and help them along. Some of the techniques in this chapter may seem disconcerting, even unnecessary, at first, but the benefits will become obvious and soon enough overcome any reservations you may have at the start.

Promoting Growth

Once their winter dormant period is over and rosebushes are ready to grow, they literally have at it. To realize their full potential, they must be helped along and properly coaxed toward the kinds of blooms you're after.

Unmounding. When leaflet sets begin appearing on exposed wood and the danger of frost is past, it's time to unmound. Lots has been going on under the mounds that cover newly planted bushes, and mounding materials must be removed carefully to keep from damaging tender new growth. Slow trickles from a water wand are perfect; clumps of mulch will fall from the canes, causing no damage.

If you can't use water, remove the mulch carefully with your fingers, not with your hands or a tool. New growth can be snapped off with a single false move.

Mulching. Unmounding gives you the starting materials for mulching—another maintenance step. Mulching is simply layering organic material over the soil among the bushes. In all of rose culture, nothing is more practical or more beneficial for rosebushes and the beds in which they grow.

Depending on where you've placed the bud union, you can pile mulch anywhere from two to four inches thick. I use at least three inches of mulch because I plant the bud unions that high above soil level. I can do this because I grow roses in a mild climate and don't worry about exposed bud unions being damaged in a hard winter freeze.

MULCHING

Mulching is nothing but layering organic material at the base of rosebushes. How much mulch you use depends on how high above ground you plant bud unions. I use three inches or more of mulch, and my roses benefit from a steady breakdown of nutrients all season long. Also, mulch protects roots from summer's burning rays and keeps weeds from gaining a solid footing.

Mulching makes three important contributions to rose culture. First, since the recommended watering procedure is flooding of rose beds, water flows over and through mulch each time you irrigate, slowly releasing nutrients. Mulch is organic and contains valuable nutrients that aren't available all at once. They break down steadily during growing seasons, usually reducing their bulk by half each year.

Second, mulch conserves water and provides a blanket of protection from the hard rays of the summer sun. Suggested irrigation schedules call for watering infrequently but deeply. Mulch keeps water under the soil surface.

Finally, mulching controls weeds. If mulch is thick enough, weeds can't easily grow through it. If they do, they're not difficult to remove because the soil under the mulch is friable and their roots haven't anchored themselves.

Feeder roots that develop along larger roots benefit greatly from mulch. They gobble up nutrients as soon as water leaches them from organic mulch materials.

Once you begin mulching, adding dry organic materials in the spring gets easier each year. Mulch becomes more friable, loose, and amenable to additives. It's easy to rake a circle around each bush, work in dry organic material, and cover the whole thing with fresh mulching materials for the coming season.

Manure is the single most important material, but remember that it must be aged to keep from burning the bud union and the delicate hairlike young feeder roots just beneath the soil surface. Manure has nutritional value, though an even bigger plus is the heat it generates as it decomposes. It warms the soil and boosts bacterial reactions that expedite mulch breakdown.

Another mulch material I've become sold on is alfalfa. It's readily available, inexpensive, and easy to use. Alfalfa comes either as meal or pelleted. Both work, but make sure there are no additives. I use two two-pound coffee cans full of it around each bush I either un-mound (newly planted bushes) or remulch (existing bushes). I spread alfalfa around the base of bushes and cover it with other mulch material. The reason I cover it is that its khaki green color makes alfalfa look like foreign matter compared to other mulch materials, which are usually some shade of brown. If you don't find it unsightly until it, too, turns brown, don't cover it and watch how quickly it breaks down.

As it disintegrates, alfalfa yields an alcohol called tricontenal to which roses take a particular shine. When it reaches their roots, roses act as though they've been aching for a stiff drink. Some claim it stimulates new basal breaks (growth from the bud union). I wouldn't care to guarantee such results, but neither would I want to deprive my bushes of an annual alfalfa feed.

Additional mulch materials can be anything organic that breaks down into humus: compost, aged bark, leaf mold, rice hulls, or peat moss. Sawdust and wood shavings are good sources for mulch bulk, but they require nitrogen to complete their own breakdown. If you have a good supply of shredded wood, just add extra nitrogen to help them break down so they won't usurp what's meant for bushes.

Lawn clippings and pine needles are also good, but they have a tendency to "mat" if they aren't mixed in well. The surface of these mats causes water runoff and interferes with irrigation.

As I mentioned earlier, we use spent mushroom compost for mulch. If we were closer to the wine country, we'd use pomace. If I lived in the Midwest, I'd look for buckwheat hulls or ground corn-cobs. In Louisiana, I'd go after bagasse. All are perfectly wonderful sources of nutritional mulch, and one may be only marginally better than another—it's their availability that matters. Look around your local area for sources of nutritious, inexpensive mulch.

If you persist in not mulching, you must do something each spring to loosen soil before you apply dry fertilizers around the base of the bushes. Soil with no blanket of mulch becomes hard and compacted, and fertilizers can't be scratched in. Compressed soil also inhibits the development of feeder roots.

Raising beds.   Anyone who has had drainage problems or who grows plants for which drainage can never be too perfect knows the advantage of raised beds. When the time comes for you to think about constructing your own, you might consider a shortcut I have discovered.

At Garden Valley Ranch we plant and mound bushes directly into the ground, with nothing around them. After unmounding, we begin adding mulch to a height that requires something to hold it in. Using inexpensive two-by-six-inch redwood cut from fallen trees, we lay lengths on edge and frame beds. Most of our beds are one hundred feet long and six feet wide, with bushes planted in pairs three feet apart. The redwood lengths are supported every five feet with a stake, and the ends are toenailed together. When the frame is completed, there is a five-inch (one inch of wood is underground, in a narrow trench) border around the entire bed, which can be filled with mulch material that won't drain away with waterings. I like to use four inches of mulch, for the nutrients it provides and to reduce weeds that would otherwise establish themselves.

Watering. You already know that roses require lots of water. What you might not know is that roses like being watered a certain way and only just so often.

Except on mornings of guaranteed warm days when you want to rid bushes of dust or spray residues, never water roses from overhead. Wet foliage invites disease.

It's more important to water deeply than to water often. Feeder roots will develop no matter how you water; it's the long roots you need to train. Encourage deep roots by forcing them down in their search for water.

The best watering method, flooding, is easy if you have raised beds. When beds are flooded, the water spreads nutrients throughout the mulch, benefiting feeder roots. With proper drainage, water reaches levels well below the soil surface, thus encouraging taproots to find it.

Water wands are good to use since they break up the flow of water passing through them. Hard spurts from an open hose will disturb mulch material and expose fragile roots.

I can't tell you how often to water because of local differences. Generalities don't apply if days have been warm or if wind robs bushes of water.

When I tell people that we water only every eight to ten days, they seem incredulous. We use raised beds and plant bushes high, since we add four inches of mulch. When we water, we flood. The carpet of mulch insures that bushes have plenty of moisture for more than a week between waterings. If a hot spell comes along or if bushes show signs of drying out, we water.

Fertilizing. Besides being big drinkers, roses like to eat a lot. They'll reward you with increased bloom for the meals you give them.

In addition to putting dry fertilizers into the almighty hole when new bushes are planted, I use dry fertilizers once per year. For the established bushes, dry fertilizers are applied in a trench raked around the drip line, that circular area of soil directly beneath the outer reaches of the tips of a pruned bush. Dry fertilizers should be applied as early in spring as sets of leaves appear. The ones I use yearly are discussed in Chapter 3.

Rake soil back over the trench after putting fertilizers in it. Water well and plan to use liquid fertilizers for the rest of the growing season.

Liquid fertilizers such as Start, Grow, and Bloom are named for what they get bushes to do. Nitrogen is most important at the start of each season to get bushes off and going. Potash is needed at the end of the year when everything already on the bush should be encouraged to mature fully and new growth shouldn't appear. Potassium is always important and is part of most formulations. Element analyses are listed on the containers of all fertilizers.

Brand names aren't important. Take advantage of sales and stock up on fertilizers if you find a good one; they keep. Follow the application rate suggested by the manufacturer. Apply liquid fertilizers along drip lines and water in well.

Some rosarians time their applications of fertilizer to coincide with what a bush has just done or is about to do. After a flush of bloom is over, for example, fertilizer is applied to get the next crop going. I believe such pat-on-the-back practices make blooms appear all at once rather than at an even pace. What bushes are doing at any particular time is irrelevant to good fertilizing. Roses should be fed at least twice a month while they're growing and blooming.

You can buy fertilizers that are rich in trace elements such as iron, zinc, copper, manganese, magnesium, calcium, sulfur, hydrogen, oxygen, and carbon. Trace elements speed growth by interacting with nutrients that have been in the soil all along but have remained inert. My experience is that trace elements do no harm. If bushes don't need them, they remain unobtrusively in the soil until called.

When people ask me what to feed their one or two rosebushes, I always tell them to use fish emulsion; it has a primary ingredient analysis of 5-0-0, rendering it incapable of damaging your plants from overdose. Every nursery I've ever seen has it, and it's inexpensive. Try different fertilizers on your roses; they'll love the variety. If you find that particular fertilizers work well, stick with them.

Controlling Growth

In response to the loving care just suggested for promoting growth, rosebushes have ways of overreacting. Some of what they do will thrill you; some won't. You must learn to spot the differences between clues to good growth and clues to bad growth as soon as they're detectable.

Finger pruning.   Well-grown rosebushes are optimistic. In the giddiness of spring, they throw out more promise of bloom than they can realistically support. The remedy, "nipping in the bud," requires no equipment other than your fingers. New growth is so supple that you won't need tools to remove it; just rub it off with your thumbs.

Bud unions need attention first. Red swellings develop and promise what you most want: main canes. But there will be too many of them. Ten or twelve new canes appearing on a bush you just pruned to six are too many.

First, rub off any buds that are growing in the middle of the bush. Next, try to anticipate whether those you leave will interfere with others as they grow. If you think everything will not be able to co-exist, rub some off.

In Chapter 8 I recommend making "knobby cuts" when you don't know where else to make a proper cut. The places where these cuts are made harbor lots of dormant eyes. When eyes start to develop, the wisdom of knobby cuts is substantiated. As with the bud union, however, there are usually too many sprouts to leave them all. Remember that the lateral on which stems grow will have to support everything you leave. If three buds appear right next to one another, it's easy to rub off the middle one and hope that the outer two will grow away from each other. If more are massed in one spot, rub off at least half of them.

Shortly after I served as a consulting rosarian for the first time, I had an experience that made me seriously wonder if I had done roses right by agreeing to give advice on them.

We had pruned the roses at Garden Valley Ranch in two weeks of rainy weather and were taking off for a well-earned vacation in the sun. Just before leaving, I helped my first student prune and told her

FINGER PRUNING
Your hands are all you need to tame spring's frisky rosebushes. Healthy plants become optimistic in their hopes of supporting growth. Remove excess growth by rubbing off some buds with your thumb.

I'd call sometime during the next month to see how her bushes were bouncing back.

When I checked in, she told me she had been so alarmed when all the new growth on her bushes came out crimson that she had cut away all the red she could see and then fertilized. I almost dropped the phone. I had become so accustomed to the new growth on rosebushes that I had forgotten I once didn't know it was red.

I felt so terrible about not forewarning her that I went over as soon as I hung up the phone. Fortunately she had removed only the first growth, and the bushes recovered.

Rosebushes present seasonal colors out of order, with shades of red on spring growth that look like a New England fall. Even mahogany red foliage will green in plenty of time before blooms appear.

Removing blind and vegetative growth. I considered omitting a discussion of blind growth because it's so difficult to describe, much less conquer, but I couldn't stand the thought of your worrying why something that looks so right doesn't bloom.

Who knows why, but every now and then growth develops that looks as if it's going to result in a bloom but doesn't. It's called "blind" when it keeps developing without producing any buds.

The problem is determining whether growth is indeed blind. Some varieties are tricky and show buds late in the stem development. Others produce buds at funny angles or at spots where you're not used to looking.

The best thing to do is to compare carefully what you think is blind to what you know isn't. If a budless stem has developed that is distinctly longer than all the other stems on the bush that already have buds, pinch it back to a set of leaflets pointing in the right direction.

Disbudding. Buds are removed for a one-to-a-stem bloom or for sprays, depending on which is considered more beautiful for each rose variety.

One-to-a-stem disbudding is mostly for hybrid teas. Some roses produce only one bud, as if they know that's how they're prettiest. Others produce one large bud at the end of a stem and smaller buds just beneath, usually two.

The terminal bud is the large one you want to leave. Side buds should be removed when they get to be about one-fourth inch long.

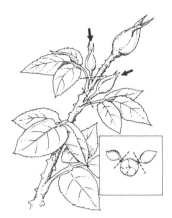

DISBUDDING
Disbud for the bloom formation that suits both you and the varieties you grow. If blooms are prettiest one to a stem, pinch out the side buds as soon as you see them developing and direct all energy to the terminal (main) bud. If a bush likes to bloom in sprays, and you too like masses of blooms, pinch out the terminal bud, which otherwise will open before everything else.

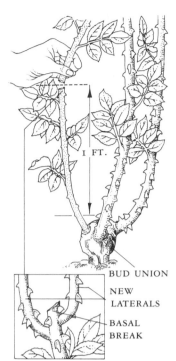

I FT.

BUD UNION

NEW
LATERALS

BASAL
BREAK

SNAPPING BASAL BREAKS
If growth coming from the bud union is left to develop on its own, it will form an unmanageable candelabra of blooms on a stem too thick to cut. Rather than let this happen, **snap basal breaks** *when they are about one foot tall. Instead of inferior blooms on an unwieldy stalk, you'll be rewarded with at least one long-stemmed rose growing on a good-size lateral. You may get two, even three!*

At that length, they can be grasped at the base and snapped off close to the stem without leaving a stub. Be sure to hold onto the terminal bud when you make these succulent snaps; you wouldn't want to end up with it in the palm of your hand.

No matter what you do, the terminal bud will continue to develop and open long before weaker side buds. Take side buds out early and direct all energy to the terminal bud. If you're thinking about having as much bloom as possible after you cut and want to leave side buds, forget it; they'll never open off the bush.

Disbudding for sprays is the opposite of disbudding for one to a stem. Terminal buds are removed and side buds are left to develop. Terminal buds left in sprays will develop fully and open before side buds have a chance. If varieties look better in sprays, remove terminal buds and channel energy into the spray formation.

Generally, hybrid teas are disbudded for one-to-a-stem blooms and floribundas and grandifloras are disbudded for sprays. There are exceptions, especially when varieties have been misclassed. You might experiment with reversing the disbudding procedures, if for no other reason than to satisfy yourself which looks better. You may decide that you like some hybrid teas in sprays and certain floribundas or grandifloras one to a stem.

One Saturday morning, a rosarian I know launched a massive disbudding attack on his rose garden. As he pinched off buds from one bush then another, his five-year-old daughter was right at his side, asking him why he was doing it this way now and another way next time. The question held no importance for her, nor did the answer—it was being with her daddy that mattered.

About halfway through the garden, he got a call from his office and had to leave. When he returned home some hours later, his daughter greeted him with the news that she had "finished the roses" for him. At first, he was still distracted by other matters and paid little attention. Then, he told me, the probable meaning of her words began to register, and he rushed out to the garden. No one-to-a-stem versus spray decisions had slowed her down. He swears she didn't miss a single bud.

Handling basal breaks.   Rose wood comes in three sizes. The largest, called basal breaks, or main canes, is new growth from the bud union. Next are laterals that develop from canes. Finally, stems develop on laterals. Apply the same rules for cutting all three anytime you cut to maintain bushes.

In the interest of shaping bushes and promoting new growth in the right direction, cuts sloping 45 degrees toward the center of the bush are made a quarter inch above evidence of dormant bud eyes, those red swellings that appear on rose wood throughout the growing season.

Basal breaks require a special treatment that may be painful for you at first, but not after you witness the rewards. If basal breaks are allowed to develop all on their own, they produce a candelabra of bloom on a thick stalk and may be so heavy that you have to stake them. The main problem, however, is that they're unwieldy and produce inferior blooms. To prevent this and to get a dividend, do what rosarians call "snapping." When new main canes are twelve to fifteen inches tall, pinch them back a few inches. New growth is so pliable it can literally be snapped off. Until you get a natural feel for snapping by hand, I suggest using shears and making cuts at the tried-and-true spot above a leaflet pointing away from the center of the bush.

Snapping does wonderful things. First, it makes what would have been a candelabra a manageable long-stemmed rose growing on a lateral. Also, because the bush is so frisky with the vigor of new growth, a second lateral soon develops just under the first. Third lateral breaks sometimes appear. Even if you don't get three, two are surely better than one.

Spotting suckers. New rose growth should stem from the bud union or above it, not from below. Growth from beneath the bud union is from rootstock, the rose variety grafted to the hybrid. Rootstock should remain underneath the soil where you planted it, concentrating its energies on massive root development. But every now and then, from sheer vigor, "suckers" break through the soil and grow as though they're something you want.

Since it looks a lot like the hybrid growth, sucker growth can fool you. When something keeps getting taller and never blooms, even when it towers above the rest of the bush, you'll realize it has tried to sucker you. If it does happen to blossom, the blooms won't be attractive, and they'll be distinctly different from those of the hybrid.

To remove sucker growth properly, you must find its point of origin on the rootstock. Don't cut it off at ground level, or it will just

SUCKERS
Sucker growth *develops below the bud unions. Since it comes from the rootstock, not from the hybrid you planted for, take it out as soon as you spot it. To remove it properly, dig beneath the soil to find the point of origin and cut it off flush. When cut above ground, suckers just grow back.*

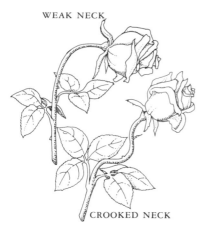

WEAK NECK

CROOKED NECK

**WEAK AND CROOKED
NECKS**
*Several fine rose varieties are
plagued with* **weak necks**
*that can't hold their blooms
erect.* **Crooked necks** *are
another matter; they're not
weak at all, they just didn't
grow straight. Some rose varieties have stems shaped like a
swan's neck, but they proudly
display their blossoms.*

grow back. Dig under the soil with your fingers until you find the point from which it emanates and cut it off flush, with no stub.

Right after I had learned about snapping new canes, I noticed a particularly vigorous one on a bush of Peace. I let it get about fourteen inches high, then I proudly snapped the new "cane" and watched for development. When it began to grow faster than the rest of the bush, I was certain I had found the secret to increasing blooms and was embarrassed when I realized I had been giving loving attention to something I should have cut out the moment I had first seen it. I'm still fooled sometimes, but less often now that I check where new growth comes from and carefully compare foliage patterns to make sure that new canes produce leaves like those on the rest of the bush.

Knowing necks. The neck (peduncle, in rose anatomy) is that portion of stem just beneath the bloom, down to the first bract of foliage. Besides those that grow straight, two kinds of necks are notable.

Weak necks are unable to keep blooms erect. Blossoms bend over and nod. Weak necks occur mostly in varieties that have extra-large blooms and stems that can't support them.

I don't mind all weak necks. I know rosarians who prefer them because they prove their blooms are large. Something about that seems a bit off to me, but you'll never get me to hand over my bushes of Helen Traubel or Charlotte Armstrong, both of which nod in a wonderfully decadent way. Nodding blooms are perfect for some kinds of display. On a high kitchen shelf or dining room ledge, they'll look right down at you. Crooked necks aren't weak at all; they just don't grow straight. Crooked necks are typical of some worthy varieties and shouldn't be considered a fault. Even when bent like a swan's, a strong neck can hold a bloom erect.

Once when I was still exhibiting, I noticed some days before a show that a bloom of Bewitched was developing nicely. Bewitched is one of those roses that produces a lot of crooked but strong necks. When show day rolled around, the bloom was perfect, but I realized that I could neither straighten nor conceal the very crooked neck. Somehow I thought it wouldn't matter. Neither did the judges—they hung a first prize ribbon around its droopy nape.

Living with croppers. Rose varieties that produce all their blooms in one giant flush are said to "come a cropper" and are generally less desirable than roses that stagger blooms.

Croppers make bushes seem alive with bloom, but unless you need a lot at once, you'll probably prefer varieties that pace bloom more evenly.

Once in a while, of course, you will need a lot of blooms from one bush at the same time. I remember a young woman who came to Garden Valley Ranch and told me that she wanted just a few roses for her wedding the next day, but that she'd like them all of one light pink variety. She couldn't have come at a worse time; the day before we had filled a large order for pinks of every shade and had cut everything in sight.

As it happened, however, we had hybridized a rose that needed further improvement. One of its problems was that blooms came all at once. I remembered that it was flowering in the hybridizing area, from where we don't sell blooms.

When I took her to see the bush, the young bride-to-be said the color was perfect. It had eighteen blooms and buds, exactly the number she needed. I knew it meant I wouldn't have another bloom for hybridizing from that bush for six to eight weeks. Even so, I cut off every one for her—somehow her wedding seemed more important than our cross-pollinations.

Eliminating Growth

During a season, uninvited growth can appear on bushes. You didn't want it to begin with, and there's no need to keep it around.

Cutting out dieback.   A rosarian could go gray trying to figure out what causes dieback. Classically, dieback occurs when any rose wood is cut at the wrong place. Stems start to die in a downward direction and keep dying until the spot is reached where a proper cut should have been made in the first place. Sometimes it won't stop even there, progressing instead all the way to the bud union. If you find it in time, a proper cut made somewhere below the dead wood will save the cane. You must act the moment you spot dieback. Even if you cut stuff you'd love to keep, get it out before it spreads.

I hate telling you this, but there can also be die "up." I haven't the faintest clue to its cause. All of a sudden dead areas will appear in the middle of an otherwise healthy cane. Since the disease will be moving upward, you might as well cut below the spot as soon as you see it and stop wasting the bush's time; it can't rejuvenate and will waste energy trying.

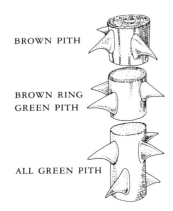

BROWN PITH

BROWN RING
GREEN PITH

ALL GREEN PITH

DIEBACK
Cut out **dieback** *as soon as you see dead areas on the outer reaches of canes or laterals. To arrest dieback (or dieup), keep cutting until you find greenish white pith with no brown rings.*

At least it's easy to tell when you've cut away enough. If dieback or dieup is present, you'll see brown rings within the pith of the wood you cut away. As long as you see brown, keep cutting. When you reach the point of healthy greenish white pith with no brown rings, dieback or dieup has been arrested.

Taking off yellowed foliage.   Leaves will yellow either from age or to signal a bush's need, usually for iron or nitrogen. When green leaves yellow, they're of little use to the plant. Too much energy will be spent trying to make them well, and it won't work. Get rid of them as soon as you're convinced they're permanently yellow; they won't turn green again.

The first leaves to yellow are at the bottoms of bushes. Here's a chance to kill two birds with one stone. When you remove yellowing leaves from the lower part of the bush, you simultaneously discourage spider mites, which get their start on leaves close to the ground. By midsummer I have often removed all leaves on the bottom quarter of the bushes. Air circulation is improved and sprays of water during irrigation discourage insects.

Getting over poor performers.   Of all writers on gardening, Vita Sackville-West has had the strongest influence on me. She became an avid gardener and wrote about it out of sheer enthusiasm. Her novels and poetry collections were well received, but for my money her best writing was on the cultivation of flowers. Many of Ms. Sackville-West's theories have made lasting impressions on me, but one is indelible.

If a rose, or any garden plant for that matter, doesn't perform well, said Ms. Sackville-West, get rid of it. Replace it with something that has either already proven itself or shows all likelihood of it.

Roses deserve a two-year test. I have grown varieties that performed poorly the first year, then lived up to my expectations the second year and thereafter. But I have never grown a rose that took more than two years to get me to like it if I was ever going to. After two years, bushes that don't make the grade should be pruned with a shovel.

Three Needless Fears

I shied away from three aspects of good maintenance when I started growing roses. If I can spare you the needless fears I suffered, you and your roses will be happier for it.

Installing an irrigation system. When I grew only a few roses, I insisted that I liked the time I spent hand-watering my garden. It was true. What I didn't realize was that if I had installed an automatic irrigation system, I could have spent that same time inspecting and admiring everything while bushes were being watered, without having to stand around holding a hose. Irrigation systems are a godsend. They're efficient, a snap to install, and inexpensive.

Water can be emitted to suit how wet you want areas around bushes. Drip systems can be used without so much as dampening soil surfaces. I'm not in favor of drip irrigation not because I don't believe it works, but rather because it releases water at pinpoints and thus can't take advantage of mulch. If mulch doesn't get thoroughly soaked, nutritional values aren't released. I use a water emitter that produces a microjet spray of water in a full five-foot circle, and I space my emitters so that rose beds get completely drenched.

After you find that you can water automatically, you have yet another pleasant surprise when you learn that you can fertilize at the same time. Fertilizer dispensers can work in conjunction with watering. Put full strength into dispensers, liquid fertilizers are automatically diluted for desired release strengths.

Irrigation specialists are listed in the yellow pages. Materials are readily available, cheap, and easy to put together with special adhesives that are brushed onto plastic pipes. Shapes are available for all garden contours.

Analyzing soil. At first, soil analyses seemed unworkable to me. I was convinced that while knowing my soil's pH might be interesting, soil analyses were really superfluous because I knew I was starting with good soil and adding proven nutrients. Later on I had another reason for skipping a soil analysis: my soil had become so complex because of the many additives I gave it that there would be no one spot where I could get a truly representative sample.

Once I gave in and decided to investigate pH, this latter excuse caved in. Soil analysis experts tell you exactly how to get multiple soil samples, the total of which will provide a true sample of what you're growing in.

Tell analyzers what you grow, take their instructions for getting samples, and follow their advice to the letter. You'll be amazed at how easy it is to add what you lack, and how inexpensively you can correct for improper soil pH. The final rewards are blooms you never imagined you could produce.

This is the time to consider trace elements. You may learn that something missing entirely is easy to add. When you do supply the missing element, the results can be staggering as nutrients that have been present all along but lying dormant are released.

Composting.   I always thought composting was messy. It was something for those who were a little too far gone on organic gardening. I didn't change my mind until I began to feel guilty about filling large trash cans with perfectly healthy foliage, a wonderful source of nutrients that I had cut off bushes or blooms. I read up on composting and learned that I was tossing out other valuable nutrients when I disposed of kitchen scraps such as eggshells, vegetable peelings, melon rinds, even coffee grounds.

Small gardens don't have space for a compost pile, but self-contained composting containers are available and work well. If you have enough space, composting works perfectly right on top of the soil, and the pile can be kept neat and odorless.

Now we keep a compost pile that resembles something you'd expect to see in Chichén Itzá—broad at the base and narrowing toward the top. Everything taken from the roses is used unless it's diseased. Even prunings are shredded along with foliage and stems and added to kitchen scraps. Breakdown is accelerated by layering shredded material with fresh chicken manure. When we remulch rose beds each year, we use composted salvage from the previous season.

Once when I was ordered to bed with the flu, I read about good things to add to a compost pile. Incredibly rich sources are all around us. For instance, feathers have a chemical analysis of 15.30-0-0, and waste from a felt hat factory boasts 13.80-0-.98.

I can't tell you how to compost on anything but a large scale. To learn how you can do it in the space you have available, read *Let It Rot* by Stu Campbell.

Unfortunately, no amount of good maintenance will control insects and fungus diseases. For those, you must learn about spraying.

CHAPTER 5
Spraying

If I could find varieties of modern roses that never contracted diseases or attracted bugs, I'd happily omit this chapter. If there were no such thing as mildew to turn leaves white or rust to color them orange or hosts of other garden gourmets waiting to devour your succulent bushes, I'd skip ahead to the more alluring sections on cutting and exhibiting.

But I can't skip this chapter, and you can't skip spraying.

The perfect climate or terrain for growing roses doesn't exist. Every spot has soil, temperature, moisture, or vegetation that will encourage some of the many rose scourges to wreak havoc on your garden if you don't get there first.

Fungus Diseases

These head the list. The big three of these depressing afflictions are mildew, rust, and blackspot. How severe they are will depend on where you live. For instance, I've never (knock on wood) had blackspot in San Francisco or Petaluma, but I've sure dealt with my share of mildew and rust.

Mildew is the worst of the fungi for me, and it probably will be for you; it seems to transcend locale. Classically, it's caused by warm days and cool nights, but less obvious weather extremes can produce it also. Mildew thrives in overcrowded plantings and in damp shady gardens where air circulation is poor.

Crinkling leaves with no color changes are the first sign of mildew. Then small round patches of mold appear and later become powdery areas of fungus filaments that harbor spores. Mildew appears on foliage, stems, thorns, or on everything.

Rust, well described by its name, appears on the undersides of leaves as reddish orange pustules that look like warts. Left unchecked, rust will work its way to leaf topsides and eventually defoliate the entire bush. Moist conditions such as winter rains, summer fogs, and heavy dew bring on rust. Supposedly, leaf surfaces must remain wet for four hours for spores to germinate.

Rust disappears during hot summer spells since spores can't survive temperatures in excess of 80 degrees for longer than a week. Insects, wind, and rain spread the disease spores, most rapidly when fallen leaves are allowed to dampen.

Blackspot occurs mostly in humid weather and in areas of abundant summer rainfall. Blackspot affects both sides of leaves with black rings that may be surrounded by yellow fringes. As the fungus develops, leaves may lose all their green and turn yellow. Rain or watering will accelerate its spreading, and its spores live through winters if they remain in cane lesions or on fallen leaves.

Insects

Aphids are usually green but also can be reddish brown. Whatever their color, they're tiny, soft-bodied, disgusting creatures that appear in congested numbers on tender rose growth and buds and suck on everything in sight.

Thrips are microscopic winged insects with a color preference; they're partial to whites and pastels. Thrips are suspected when buds that seem on the brink of beauty suddenly collapse with brown-flecked petals. To see thrips you have to break a bloom apart and shake its petals over a white cloth while looking for quick, tiny movements.

Mites are microscopic ($\frac{1}{75}$ inch in diameter) spiders that are usually red, although some are green or yellow. The spider mite's calling card is a web left underneath leaves at the bottom of a bush. These pests suck leaf juices, rendering foliage a dry red, yellow, brown, or gray. Hot, humid weather and poor air circulation create fertile conditions for mite infestation.

Unfortunately, the diseases and insects I've just described don't exhaust the list. I haven't mentioned diseases such as crown gall, canker, and botrytis, or insects such as whitefly and rose midge. That's because I've never dealt with them, and with luck you probably won't either. There's a full discussion of these and more garden scourges in *Compendium of Rose Diseases* by Kenneth Harst. To get a copy, send fifteen dollars to APS Books, 3340 Pilot Knob Road, St. Paul, Minnesota 55121.

I learned a hard lesson about insects peculiar to an area when I moved my rose growing from San Francisco to Petaluma. One day I came in from the field clutching a bug in my fist, exclaiming that I didn't know there were green ladybugs. There aren't. I had seen my first *Diabrotica*, better known as cucumber beetle.

Cucumber beetles go right for the kill—the bloom. What's more, they fly and they reproduce themselves in a matter of days. It's not easy to eradicate cucumber beetles, but when you see your blooms being nibbled away before your very eyes, you learn how.

Disease-Resistance

A. T. "Buddy" Harrelson of Louisiana writes in the 1984 *American Rose Annual*:

> By the way, I don't believe healthy plants resist diseases or insects. In fact, it would seem to me that bugs would thrive better on healthy plants. I can imagine one bug signaling to another . . . "Hey! C'mon over here! The chlorophyl is fine." However, a healthy plant will recover more quickly should it sustain damage.

This makes sense to me, including bugs' preference for good-looking plants. I also agree with Buddy that healthy bushes recover more quickly from whatever attacks them than do their sickly cousins.

Some rose experts believe, however, that susceptibility to mildew can be predicted by how the foliage looks. Leathery, glossy leaves, proponents claim, are less prone to mildew than dull, soft ones. When I first heard this theory, I pooh-poohed it. Now I'm not so sure.

If you asked me quickly to name a rose that mildews, I'd say Garden Party, definitely a rose with dull foliage. We keep Garden Party at Garden Valley Ranch as a "standard" for mildew. If the albino fungus is anywhere in sight, it will find Garden Party.

If I were asked to name a rose that doesn't mildew, Cathedral comes to mind. It has particularly glossy, leathery foliage. There may well be something to this theory of foliage clues, and I intend to experiment with it. In the meantime, I suggest that you check locally to learn how disease-resistance manifests itself.

Is Spraying Dangerous?

The chemical sprays used for modern roses can be dangerous. Don't think they can't. Read the labels. It's all there—dosage limits, temperature constraints, warnings to prevent skin contact and inhalation, antidotes, and more, depending on each material's relative toxicity. Sprays can affect vision if they get in your eyes, or alter your breathing if you inhale a mighty shot of their mist. Sprays can travel considerable distances and still do harm. The safety precautions on those labels are there for a good reason. Read them carefully and follow them to a T.

If You Elect Not to Use Chemical Sprays

I think that chemical sprays can be safe if handled carefully, but you may not agree. If you would rather not use them, you have some alternatives.

Use organic spray materials; they'll work to discourage some insects. Just be prepared to expend more energy than those of us who use chemicals, because organic treatments must be applied more frequently.

Sprays of agricultural soap have long been known to combat aphids and crawling insects, but they must be applied at least every four to five days. Also, they leave a coating of unappealing soapy residue.

Members of the onion family can discourage insects. When I had only a few roses, I planted garlic around the bushes, and I believe it really did discourage aphids.

Plain water is temporarily effective for discouraging mites. Spiders can't take a fine misting of water and will leave the area, but only for a few days.

Grow the hardiest modern roses you can and be satisfied with their blooms even when diseases and insects take their inevitable toll. Unless you live in a disease-prone area or are heavily infested with insects known to chew blossoms, you can get some wonderful blooms, especially early in the growing season. Later, foliage will mildew, rust, or blackspot, but blooms miraculously will still appear.

Grow some older varieties that are less prone to disease than modern introductions. I'm just now learning about old roses, and I like what I see. Old rose varieties will never replace modern roses for me, but their disease-resistance is most appealing. They're not disease-*free*, mind you; many varieties are as vulnerable as anything modern.

We grow some old rose varieties at Garden Valley Ranch and intersperse them with their modern relatives. Blanc Double de Coubert, a great pure white rose of the *Rugosa* species, was planted in our fragrant garden, where plants are grown for use in potpourri. This particular rose is very fragrant and produces beautiful red hips in the fall. Since no spray materials are used in the fragrant garden, we have the setting for a true disease-resistance test.

When foggy nights followed warm days, the white curse of mildew did appear, but was never widespread. If we had tried not spraying our modern roses only a few hundred feet away, most would have turned white as snow.

If You Do Spray—How Often?

I spray roses every ten days from April until mid-October. Your annual schedule may be slightly different, depending on where you live. I've tried to skip spraying once or twice, but have learned conclusively that if I do, rose beds begin to look like insect delicatessens or white fallout areas. Then I'll have to spend a lot of time with corrective, not preventive, spray materials. So I don't let up.

The good news is that proper spraying, including taking all necessary precautions, takes much less time than you may imagine. The garden at my house in San Francisco, where I now have one hundred bushes growing in a 25-foot-by-40-foot area, can be sprayed in slightly more than an hour. For the rewards spraying brings, that's not a lot of time to spend every ten days.

Which Sprays Should You Use?

Ten years ago the chemical division of Chevron revolutionized spraying for the home gardener by introducing Funginex, a liquid spray that treats mildew, rust, and blackspot in one fell swoop. Imagine how welcome Funginex was to thousands of overworked rosarians who previously had used three separate chemicals to achieve the same fungicidal prevention.

Funginex was a major breakthrough, but of course rosarians still had to add insecticides and miticides if they were needed. Then a few years later Chevron eliminated even this step when it began to market Orthinex, a material that combined Funginex with an insecticide and a miticide. Finally there was truly an all-in-one spray.

Orthinex is undeniably a wonderful labor-saving product, but I have a reservation about it that I'd like to share with you. I think we should spray to *prevent* fungus and *eradicate* pests. On the one hand, mildew, rust, and blackspot are always lurking around the corner, and preventive spraying must continue whether there is evidence of fungus or not. On the other hand, no amount of preventive spraying will keep away some bugs. If you spray for pests when there are none, you burden the plant with unnecessary spray materials. Eradication is for getting rid of what you see. If an insecticide or miticide isn't needed, don't use Orthinex.

Not all of the creatures that crawl over your rosebushes are enemies. Ladybugs and praying mantises, for instance, thrive on the very same insects you spray to eradicate. If you indiscriminantly use insecticides and miticides, you'll wipe out the good along with the bad.

Insects or mites in your area might not respond to the insecticide and miticide Orthinex contains. You *must* check with your consulting rosarian to learn (1) which pests are indigenous to your area, and (2) which spray materials work best on them. Also, this might be a good time to get to know your local county agricultural agent since he or she is often aware of the very latest spray materials.

Once you learn what is required to spray effectively, add those materials to Funginex. You may find they're already included in Orthinex, in which case you should revel in getting to use a single truly all-inclusive spray material.

Additional spray materials come in liquids and wettable powders. Use liquids whenever possible. Powders are messy, difficult to distribute evenly, and likely to leave an unsightly residue.

Once after I had repeatedly complained that my spraying didn't seem as effective as it should be, a consulting rosarian I often turned to reluctantly told me that I might try something he did. "Add a couple of teaspoons of vinegar to your spray materials," he said. When I pressed for the rationale, knowing his reluctance to advocate an unproven theory, he told me that when the pH of water is too high, the effectiveness of spray materials is shortened. Adding vinegar lowers water's pH. It did the trick for me, and I've never omitted vinegar from spray materials since. If you wonder about the acidity of your water, ask your local water department about its pH. If it's higher than 7.5, try adding vinegar to your spray formula. Be sure it's the first ingredient you add; if you put it in last, it tends to curdle everything else.

Sprayers

You should decide which sprayer to use after you think carefully about how much weight you're willing to lift and carry around.

Handheld sprayers work perfectly well. They're a bit of a pain when it comes to reducing spray material portions to suit their small capacity, but you may decide it's worth it for their light weight. Besides, you can mix the total amount you'll need in a larger container and refill the sprayer as it empties.

I know a woman who uses identical soft plastic spray holders to moisten her clothes for ironing and to spray her roses (she never interchanges the two). She bought both sprayers for under $2.00.

Tank sprayers range in capacity from two to five gallons. The same handle you use to pump the sprayer doubles as a carrying handle, or as a shoulder strap if you want to transfer weight to your back. The spray nozzle is at the end of a metal wand, connected to the tank by a rubber hose. Tank sprayers are more expensive than handheld models, but they're still cheap. If you take care of them and rinse container tanks after each use, they will outlive most of your bushes.

Backpack sprayers hold from three to seven gallons of spray material. If your pelvis can take the weight, they're advantageous since both hands are free. Spray material is compressed with air by pumping the tank with a metal handle that can be attached on either side— if you do a lot of spraying, it's nice to be able to switch hands for pumping. The nozzle and tank attachment are the same as for pump sprayers.

Larger containers require engines and container tanks with built-in agitators. We use a fifty-gallon commercial model pulled by a tractor for spraying the field at Garden Valley Ranch, and we're just about to outgrow it.

Sprayers with electric motors are worth considering. You won't wear yourself out pumping, and some models are designed to produce particularly fine mists of spray that cover foliage completely.

No matter which size sprayer you get, make sure the part that holds spray materials is made of one of the modern plastics. Except for stainless steel, metal tanks corrode and flake off into liquid spray material. The size of your sprayer doesn't matter if your technique is right. The woman I mentioned who uses the handheld sprayer does a better job spraying her bushes, because of her technique, than do many rosarians I know who use expensive motorized sprayers.

Technique

Rosebushes have to be misted with spray materials for effective coverage. All sprayers, from handheld to commercial models, are capable fortunately of emitting fine mist sprays.

SPRAYING TECHNIQUE
The technique you employ for spraying your roses is as important as the chemicals you use. Start spraying at the base of bushes, where infestations begin, and work toward the top. When you're through spraying upward, one downward shot will finish the job.

The method of application is important. Proper technique requires first spraying the undersides of leaves, where disease begins, starting at the bottom of the bush and working toward the top.

Since mists of spray are being directed upward, a constant "fallout" drifts down and covers the tops of the leaves. When you reach the top of the bush with your upward movement, most foliage surfaces will already be covered. One or two downward shots of spray material will finish the job.

Keep spray materials agitated to prevent settling and separation. Unless you use a power model with a built-in agitator, you must keep remixing the materials yourself. Handheld sprayers are easy; just shake them often. As sprayers get larger, they become more difficult to shake. If you carry one over your shoulder or as a backpack, you might try a technique used by an 82-year-old friend of mine. When she sprays her bushes, she wears a pocket-size clip-on radio with ear inserts. She likes to listen to country and western music, and she two-steps and waltzes through the garden, agitating her spray materials all the while.

Your goal should be to spray everything on a rosebush except the blooms. Don't aim for blooms unless you're spraying for something that attacks them specifically, such as thrips. Be forewarned, however, that you can't keep all spray material off them. If a bloom is close to the stage of openness that suits you, cut it before you spray. Otherwise, spray will discolor the blossoms. Some spray materials have a way of spreading unevenly. If you use one of these noncovering formulas, you must add a "spreader sticker" to the liquid spray to insure even foliage coverage. Commercial spreader stickers are available, but mild household detergent works perfectly well.

One of the first consulting rosarians I met gathered his protégés one Sunday afternoon to teach us effective spray technique. This otherwise gentle man had a way of furrowing his brows if one even *looked* as if one might fail to heed his advice. We saw him spray several bushes as he lectured on the importance of complete foliar coverage. To drive the point home, he said decisively, "If you skip any part of the bush, you might as well not spray at all." As he said it, he turned from a bush and looked at all of us, but his eyes fixed on *me* as though I, if anyone, would be the one to cut corners. I remember squirming, but the advice has stuck.

Tips for Safe Handling of Spray Materials

Store spray materials away from everything else, preferably behind locked doors out of reach of children and pets.

Leave chemicals in their original containers with labels intact. If you change containers and think you'll remember the recommended dosage forever, you're wrong.

Wear rubber gloves and goggles while mixing and applying materials. Make sure your clothes cover you completely, leaving no body parts exposed.

Never use spray materials in a solution stronger than that suggested by the manufacturer.

Mix materials in an open area to keep fume inhalation at a minimum. It is a good idea to wear a respirator during the mixing as well as during the spraying.

Try to spray on calm days to prevent spray drift. If wind can't be avoided, spray from the windward side.

Find a safe, out-of-the way spot where you can pour unused spray materials on the ground. Don't pour them down drains.

Wash up immediately after using spray materials.

See Chapter 8 for a discussion of dormant spray.

You'll bless your effective spray program when you start cutting blooms with foliage that complements them. At last the fun begins.

CHAPTER 6
Cutting

If you've followed my advice so far, you have some good-looking rose blooms on your hands. It would be a shame not to get a long life from them once you cut them from the bush. If you follow the advice in this chapter, you will.

Shears

We rosarians will lend you any tool but our shears. We use them for everything—for pruning, clipping, cutting. We can't walk through the garden without them because we never know when we're going to see something that has to come off right now, before it gets worse or before we forget where it is. Blind growth must be removed as soon as it is spotted, interior growth that is threatening to damage a bloom must be cleared, and broken stems need immediate removal.

Shears must be kept sharp so that clean cuts can be made. First, buy shears that *can* be sharpened, not those that "never need sharpening," for they will. I hate admitting that I paid to have my shears sharpened and oiled for the first few years I grew roses. I knew that I should be doing it myself, but I'm generally so clumsy with my hands that I feared it was one of those tasks I couldn't master.

This time I was wrong. I'm proud to say that I now have the sharpest shears around, and keeping them that way myself is a piece of cake. All you need is a soft Arkansas sharpening stone, which you can get at any nursery or hardware store, and a can of all-purpose household oil. Drag the cutting edge of the shears lightly over the stone the way you would a knife over a honing steel. You'll work out the right motion for sharpening by following the contour of the blade as you rake it across the stone. Apply the oil to the sharpening stone as you go. The stone is porous and without the oil won't glide easily along the cutting edge of the shears. By the time you finish, the oil will have spread evenly over the cutting edges, facilitating cutting.

It's wise to have a single pair of shears with which you cut blooms, maintain bushes, and prune. Find one pair that will do all these things well, keep them sharp, and always store them in the same place so that you don't mislay them. Shears should be comfortable to hold and easy to work. The ones I prefer are on the heavy side of average weight. Anything lighter seems flimsy.

You'll be surprised and confused when you shop for shears; there are so many! Not only are there all sizes, but shears come in various shapes and for stated purposes. I finally settled on one I like best—Felco No. 2. I'm fairly nationalistic and buy American products whenever I have a reasonable option, but I move camp to Switzerland when it comes to shears. We use them for every cut made at Garden Valley Ranch except at pruning time when extra-thick canes require loppers. They're not cheap (none of the good ones are), but they'll last a lifetime if properly cared for.

Cut-and-Hold Shears

After telling you that you need only one pair of shears, now I'm going to contradict myself to say there is one wonderful specialty type to get if you have enough blooms to justify the extravagance, or if you just want to add a touch of luxury to your late-afternoon cutting sessions.

I first saw cut-and-hold shears when I visited the International Flower Market in Aalsmeer, Holland. Once again the Swiss go to the head of the class with this invention. When you use them to cut a rose, the rose, stem and all, stays caught in the blades until you release the handle. The great advantage is that your other hand is free to hold the container into which blooms are dropped.

When to Cut

Rosebushes begin drawing in moisture with the first hint of approaching dusk, and they hold it until the morning light gets strong. Since you want blooms with as much moisture in them as possible, cut either before midmorning or after midafternoon.

We cut all roses in the late afternoons at Garden Valley Ranch simply because it's more convenient than in the morning. When summer days are long, we begin cutting after 5:00 P.M. even though we face thousands of cuts each evening. As the days grow shorter, particularly after the loss of daylight savings, we begin earlier. All you really want to avoid is cutting during midday, especially during

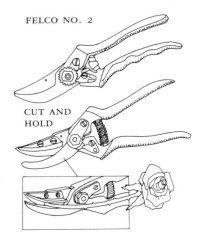

FELCO NO. 2

CUT AND HOLD

SHEARS
Rosarians can't function without shears such as **Felco No. 2**, *which they use for many rose chores—clipping, cutting, and pruning. If you want to do yourself a favor, also buy some* **cut-and-hold** *shears, which will hold a blossom against its cutting edge until you're ready to release the handle and drop the bloom wherever your free hand wants it. Use cut-and-hold shears only for cutting blooms.*

hot weather, when blooms are limp. The hour of the day at which roses are cut from their bushes is actually far less important than the conditioning you give the roses after you cut them.

Stage to Cut

Blooms of each rose variety must reach a certain stage of openness before they can be cut if they're expected to open farther or fully. The safest general rule to follow is: Wait until the sepals are down.

Sepals are those leaflike coverings of rosebuds. They are easily as individual as foliage, and some are downright decorative. Most are the same color green as the foliage of the bush on which they grow, but some have red serrated edges. Sepals grow from just under the bud and join their tips over it, completely surrounding the swelling bloom. As buds develop, so do sepals, until they can contain the bloom no longer. They then begin to unfurl one by one. In some roses this unfurling is dramatic, as the sepals arch gracefully backward in brackets that seem to lend elegant architectural support to the coming bloom.

When the sepals are down and the bud has begun to open ("cracked" in florist lingo), the bloom can be cut. How far the bud must have opened before the cut is made varies from one kind of rose to another. Those varieties with fewer petals don't have to be open very far before they can be cut. As petalage increases, so does the necessary degree of bud openness. Heavily petaled roses must show a row of petals in addition to a well-defined center around which other rows of petals are developing. If you cut them before this stage, they won't open. With certain other blooms, surprisingly, the sepals needn't be down at all before you cut.

Observe the sepals closely as you cut blooms, and you'll quickly become familiar with these variations in cutting stages. You may even grow quite daring as you learn which ones can be safely cut with their sepals still tightly furled, as is the case with a black Mister Lincoln or a still-green Sweet Afton.

Where to Cut

If you commit only one fact of this chapter to memory, make it this one: Where you cut a bloom is vital to the bush it is leaving. To cut blooms at the right place, you must familiarize yourself with patterns of rose foliage.

Rose leaves usually come in sets of three, five, and seven, increas-

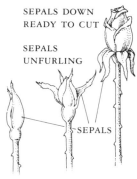

SEPALS DOWN
READY TO CUT

SEPALS
UNFURLING

SEPALS

SEPALS UP

SEPALS
Sepals grow like leaves from just under the rosebud to cover its tip. Sepals unfurl and arch downward to signal that a bloom is ready to be cut. If the sepals aren't down, or if the bud isn't "cracked," the bloom won't open after it is cut from the bush.

ing in number from the bloom downward to where its stem begins. Older or particularly healthy varieties produce nine or more leaflet sets. For this lesson, remember only *five*.

Properly cut blooms leave at least two sets of five leaflets on the stem from which they're cut. More would be nice, particularly if a newly planted bush can't yet afford to give up long stems.

Selecting the particular five-leaflet set above which to make the cut is equally important: it must point outward from the center of the bush. At the very base of leaflets and the stems from which they grow is an *axil* that reveals a swelling red bud. This dormant eye is the beginning of the rose that will bloom some six to eight weeks after you make the cut.

Once you select which five-leaflet set to cut above, make the cut one-quarter inch above the axil at a 45-degree angle with the downward slope toward the center of the bush.

CUT AT 45° TO
CENTER OF BUSH

WHERE TO CUT
What you take from a bush vitally affects what you leave behind. **Properly cut blooms** *leave at least two sets of five leaflets on the stem from which they grew. The five-leaflet set above which the cut is made should point outward from the center of the bush— the direction in which your new rose will grow.*

Cut for the Bush or the Bloom?

If you cut with the bush in mind, stem length must sometimes be sacrificed. Ideally, the bush must keep a certain shape, growing outward so that the stems don't bang into each other and don't compete for light. If no convenient five-leaflet set is facing away from the bush, or if the stem is on the short side of average and what you really want would require taking everything, then you must cut shorter stems. If a bush is very young or acting poorly, then it is wise to cut shorter stems because these bushes need all the help they can get, including the food extra leaves may generate. You'll feel better about your short-stemmed roses if you dwell on the good what you leave behind does for the rest of the bush.

If you must, you can cut for the bloom anyway if you want to enter a rose in a show and know you'll need all available stem length to have a prayer for a blue ribbon. Or you may have just purchased a new crystal bud vase that will show off the stem and foliage of your prize blooms. In those cases, I say go for it. Just acknowledge that you're being piggy and resolve not to do it more often than necessary, or bushes will wither from your greed.

Some people may have told you not to cut blooms from first-year bushes: pay no attention to such silly advice. Even though you dutifully leave a bloom on a bush because you've been told that new bushes need all the foliage possible to generate food, you must cut it off anyway when it begins to drop its petals. Otherwise, the bush thinks it's time to "go to seed" and will expend energy developing the hip, a rose's seedpod. What can possibly be gained by leaving the bloom on the bush for these extra few days, a week at most? If you planted roses for garden display, that's one thing; leave them and gain the few extra days' work from their foliage. But if you want blooms in the house, take them. Just be kind when you know you must.

Keep in mind that a new rose can have a stem only as thick as that from which it was cut. If you cut from twigs, you'll get more twigs. If you're going to be disappointed with the stem you're about to cut and see that only spindly growth will come from where the cut is made, cut back farther.

Conditioning

I've never figured out why this subject stumps some wonderful rosarians; conditioning is so easy, and it doubles the life of rose blooms.

Preservatives. Most florists staple a small soft plastic bag of preservatives to the material they wrap your flowers in. Use them; they work. When you have roses of your own, you can prepare your own effective preservatives. To one quart of lukewarm water, add one teaspoon of sugar and a few drops of household bleach. The sucrose will continue to feed the bloom for development now that it's off the bush, and the bleach will kill bacteria. This homemade concoction will work about as well as anything commercially available.

Before you cut, mix preservatives with 105-degree water in the container where you'll put the blooms. Newly cut roses quickly absorb preservatives if there's a good drink of lukewarm water to go with them.

Don't take the container of water to the garden with you when you go to cut. All you will do is compress blooms and slosh water on your feet. If cut at the right time, roses will do perfectly nicely for at least an hour without water. It's what you do *after* you cut that matters most.

Wicker baskets are nice carriers if they're long enough for the stem length you'll be getting. At Garden Valley Ranch we use 2-foot-by-3-foot laundry baskets that are only 9 inches deep; we can stack a lot of roses in them without crushing the roses.

Foliage removal is necessary to a point. Several people have made me a gift of tongs for foliar removal with instructions to press them against stems and pull downward to remove thorns and foliage. I thank them for the gift and put it away.

Foliage and thorns are so easy to snap or cut off that there's no need for a device to yank them off. If the roses aren't going to be handled, as when blooms are put into clear bud vases, leave the thorns. They're dramatic to look at, especially under water.

Foliage is another matter. I don't like looking at it under water. Even if it doesn't show, rose foliage becomes a tangled mess at the bottom of a container. This is particularly true if you arrange roses with other flowers or foliage. Remove lower leaves whether they will show or not.

Cutting stems under water is the single most important step for extending bloom life for all flowers, not just roses. When stems are cut from their bushes, they draw in air and begin to make pockets which, when they reach the bloom, cause the blossom to nod in premature death. When you recut the stems under water, they draw no air, and the water acts as a temporary sealant when stems are later moved around out of water.

Garden roses have thick pithy stems compared to the fragile ones of greenhouse roses. Cutting stems under water and using preservatives give garden roses the boost they need to fully mature.

You don't need a large container for cutting stems under water. A small bowl or saucer will do just fine. Dip the end of the stem in the water, cut one-quarter inch off at an angle, and place the stem in a container of lukewarm water with preservatives added.

Keeping roses the maximum period requires one more step, which is really a repetition of the one you have just learned. If you change a rose's water every day, recut its stem, and add fresh preservatives, it will reciprocate by lasting longer than you ever thought possible. If you haven't time to do it all, at least keep ample water in the container. Roses drink an incredible amount, and remember that they're continuing to grow because of the sugars in the preservatives. You'll be convinced when you see a bud develop into a bloom the size of a dinner plate.

There's a bud vase I'm particularly fond of because it suits my lazy ways. It's meant to hold only one rose and is bulb-shaped at the bottom, so that the rose always has ample water, even if I forget to

CUTTING STEMS UNDER WATER
*Stems cut from bushes draw air that bubbles its way to the blooms, causing them to nod in premature death. To avoid air bubbles, **recut** stems—dip their tips into a bowl of water and cut off one-quarter inch of stem. This process will insure a longer life for all your blooms, not just your roses.*

refill it. I don't pretend that roses put in this practical container will last as long as those whose stems are recut every day, but if I haven't the time to do it or have so many roses that I can't keep track, it's a welcome helper.

Hardening is another florist's term. It means that all parts of a flower, from stem to petals, have hardened to the point of maximum water retention. Flowers can take the most shock when they've been hardened.

If you need your roses right away, go ahead and use them anytime after you've cut their stems under water and put them into lukewarm water. If you have the time or want maximum bloom life, leave them in the container with the preservatives and put the container in a cool, dark spot. Ground-floor closets are ideal. By the time the water reaches room temperature, the blooms will be turgid. You'll be happy you did this as the days go by and by and your blooms last and last.

Transporting roses should include keeping them in water. Once I begin hardening a cut bloom, I like to keep it in water until it has found a home. Plastic floral buckets are nice for transporting a good number of roses. For fewer blooms, wax-coated milk and juice containers can be transported in a carrier I'll tell you about. Its base is a round of wood onto which some number of coffee cans are secured, along with a handle made from leftover pipe lengths. Wax containers can be set within the empty coffee cans and won't spill over.

Larger containers can be transported easily with the help of sand-bags. A friend of mine made sandbags for us from denim remnants; we filled them with pea gravel. They'll secure a container of any size or shape in even the most awkward corner of your vehicle.

Rain

Rain is wonderful for bushes, especially if they were about to get watered anyway. It does nothing good for the blooms, however. Once a bloom has begun to open, rain will seep in between the petals and, in time, rot the bud. Do one of two things. If you can, cut blooms before it rains. Drops of water act like tiny magnifiers of sun rays and spot petals and foliage. Even though you may have to cut some before you'd really like to, they'll open in the vase if properly cared for. Your other alternative, if you can't get to the blooms until after they've been rained on, is to hold them upside down by the tips of their stems

A ROSE CARRIER

Once rose stems have been cut and recut, they should remain in water for the rest of their days. To make transporting blooms easier, make a carrier like this one from a slab of wood, two-pound coffee cans, and plumbing leftovers. Wax-coated containers fit snugly within the cans and won't spill over in your car. Once you give away roses, you'll never have to save milk or juice cartons again; your friends will do it for you, in hopes of a refill.

right after you cut them and shake them up and down. Don't shake them sideways. If you do, especially when holding them near their necks, they'll snap off in your hands.

I know a woman who cuts her roses after rains and clothespins them upside down to her laundry line. It's true that this does the trick, but I've always suspected she enjoys watching her neighbors' reactions more than she does her drained blooms.

You'll soon realize that some of the blooms you cut are worthy of more than household use. If you have a competitive streak, why not try exhibiting them?

CHAPTER 7
Exhibiting

This chapter is not written to persuade you to exhibit, but rather to let you know what it's all about. Though I stopped competing long ago, exhibiting strongly influenced the way I grow roses. Only by knowing what judges look for in a given rose did I come to know an outstanding bloom when I produced one. I still strive to grow exhibition-quality roses, even knowing that not every bloom can possibly reach that standard and that the best of varieties will yield countless blooms that should never get *near* a show table.

Rose shows are where you get to see the varieties you probably want to grow and the quality for which you might strive. These events provide a wonderful means to view new cultivars that you may have heard about but can't decide if you want to plant. Often you'll be challenged by seeing blooms of varieties you already grow that far excel what you've been able to produce. (You'll also see blooms that aren't nearly as good as the ones you left on the bushes that very morning.)

Rules for exhibiting and divisions for entries for each competitive event are printed in a show schedule—a list of what you can and can't enter. Some events are open to all exhibitors; others specify exhibitor status (novice, amateur, advanced amateur). Show schedules can be very complicated, but basic to all are the exhibition blooms, and it is with these that we shall deal. Once you know what hybrid teas, floribundas, and grandifloras are supposed to look like, show schedules are easy to follow.

Judging Roses

As judges approach each bloom for consideration, they compare it to a picture, indelibly imprinted in their mind's eye, of the best example of that variety they have ever seen. Occasionally, judges will encounter a bloom that is better than any of its kind they remember; this image then becomes the new standard.

Point Scoring

For an experienced judge, a rose doesn't have to be analyzed in parts; it's the overall appearance that matters. For the benefit of others, however, or in case of a close call among fellow judges, a point-scoring system suggested by the American Rose Society assigns numerical values to the elements being evaluated. There is a total possible score of one hundred, with the following assignments:

Form	25 points
Color	20 points
Substance	15 points
Stem and foliage	20 points
Balance and proportion	10 points
Size	10 points

Let's look at these elements one by one.

Form (25 points)

This is the most important element. Forms of rose blooms are classified as formal or decorative, and each is judged by different standards.

Formal hybrid teas are thought to reach perfection somewhere between the half- to three-quarter-open stage. When viewing the bloom from the top, a judge will want to see, first, a well-defined, pointed center with surrounding petals unfurling in symmetrical balance. Depending upon the petalage count for each variety, further standards dictate how many rows of petals should surround the center.

These rules insure that specimens have reached a sufficient degree of openness to reveal their centers, those pinpoint landmarks around which petals unfurl. Judges must be convinced that the perfect center does, in fact, exist. Unless it's apparent, there's no basis for evaluating form.

While blooms are developing, the bud stage occurs when sepals are down and the petals have begun to unfurl. Sometimes what will eventually be the center is apparent; more often not. Buds offer no assurance of a center, and petals could be camouflaging a center you won't later be able to find with a road map. *A bud is not a bloom* and should never be exhibited except as part of a stage-of-bloom display.

EXHIBITION FORM

*Form carries more weight
(twenty-five points) than any
other element. Form is either*
exhibition *, with a high,
pointed crown rising from symmetrical rows of petals around
a bull's-eye center, or form is*
decorative *, with cupped or
ruffled blossoms that may have
flat, even sunken, centers.
Judges know how to spot blooms
typical of their varieties.*

*However blossoms are
formed, they should be carried
on* **balanced** *and* **propor-
tioned** *stems. If blooms are
large, stems should be long and
cloaked in foliage. With
smaller blossoms, stems may be
shorter, with fewer leaves.*

EXHIBITION FORM   DECORATIVE FORM   BALANCE AND PROPORTION

Judges can't touch blooms, but they can pick up the bottles or bud
vases in which the specimens are displayed to view them from different angles. Using the neck of the container as a pivotal point, blooms
are also viewed from the side to look for symmetry from that angle
and to compare the height of the center to the rest of the bloom.

Informal, or decorative, blooms differ primarily in the center they
display. These blossoms are often ruffled or cupped, with a center
that is actually sunken, although still displaying a point. The difference between these and the formal types is most evident when blooms
are viewed from the side, since decorative centers rarely rise above the
rest of the bloom. Occasionally, because of particularly good growing
or weather conditions, a decorative variety can produce a bloom that
has true formal exhibition form, including a high, pointed center.
Seeing this occur, the judge then has a new standard, and later blooms
for that variety will be subject to comparison with it.

One such decorative hybrid tea almost became a Queen for me. Pat
Martin, who started me in this madness, gave me a bush of Pink
Peace because it was her favorite rose. She liked pink, which this rose
certainly is, and she liked fragrance, which Pink Peace certainly has.
(It's also one of the few modern roses that closes its petals at night.)
The one I entered in a show on this particular day looked like a huge
fragrant cabbage, but with form. The bloom was easily eight inches
across and had a stem to go with it. No one could ignore it, especially
not the judges, who quickly ordered a blue ribbon hung around the

neck of its container. After it was declared the winner in its section, it was moved to the "Queen's Table," the holding ground for regal selection.

I was "clerking" in this particular show—it's not a bad idea to be a gofer and note-taker for judges, since they talk all the time and you can learn a lot. The pinks weren't in the section my judges were picking apart, but when we finished our assigned area, I saw the Pink Peace up there with the other blue-ribbon beauties. It was bigger than anything in sight, and I knew if the judges got close enough to it, the aroma might sway them even though fragrance isn't a legitimate factor.

It didn't win, but it retained the first prize from its section. My entry of Electron, a rose considered exemplary for exhibition form, languished in third place in the same color division.

Color (20 points)

Three components make up color: hue, chroma, and brightness. Hue is what distinguishes one color from another. Chroma determines how pure and intense the color is, and brightness is synonymous with clarity. In the judge's mind is a picture of the ideal overall color for all rose varieties. Growing conditions, weather, and refrigeration can all markedly alter color and either improve or detract from possible color-point allocation.

Unevenness of color, such as one finds in those varieties that characteristically have green or white petal streaks, results in penalties. Fortunately for the exhibitor, flaws usually occur in the outer row of petals, which can be unobtrusively removed without damaging overall symmetry and form.

Hybridizers of new roses select the color classification from seventeen color classes established by the American Rose Society:

1. White or near white	10. Pink blend
2. Medium yellow	11. Deep pink
3. Deep yellow	12. Medium red
4. Yellow blend	13. Dark red
5. Apricot blend	14. Red blend
6. Orange and orange blend	15. Mauve
7. Orange-red	16. Russet
8. Light pink	17. Mauve blend
9. Medium pink	

Substance (15 points)

This is what makes red roses look velvety or pastels look opalescent. It's petal texture. Rose blossoms with good substance have firm, crisp petals with enough moisture and starch to insure good keeping qualities. Blooms usually begin losing substance at the edges of outer petals. The moisture loss is evidenced in a "creping" effect, a change from translucency to a dull, crinkled look.

Since a rose that is losing substance will also lose color to some degree, this element counts for more than its fifteen points would suggest.

Stem and Foliage (20 points)

Stems have to be reasonably straight and of a length complimentary to the bloom. Foliage must be typical of the variety and should be undamaged, with no evidence of disease or spray residue. Show rules state that thorns cannot be removed from the portion of stem above the bud vase, but you must often remove thorns from lower sections just to get the stem into the container.

Rose leaflets come in sets of three, five, seven, or nine, with smaller clusters at the top portions of the stem and larger clusters farther down. When a judge holds a specimen so that he can look down on the bloom, he should see a symmetrical, generally circular frame of foliage that sets off the bloom.

Balance and Proportion (10 points)

Here the overall appearance of the entry is assessed for how well all the elements come together. Element harmony is the key. If a bloom is large, it must have a relatively long stem and abundant foliage. Smaller blooms require shorter stems and sparser foliage so they aren't overwhelmed. If a huge bloom is perched upon a short stem, or a small bloom upon a long one, balance and proportion will be off.

Size (10 points)

Judges resorting to point scoring would give seven to eight points for an average-size bloom from a given variety. The extra points are reserved for larger-than-usual blooms. And the bigger the better; all other things being equal, the larger blooms will always win out.

Variety Requirements

Hybrid Teas. While many rose shows will include a section for hybrid tea sprays, these blooms are almost always exhibited one per stem. Side buds mean disqualification. What is more, there should be no distracting evidence of scarring from disbudding.

Floribundas. Except in specially designated sections, floribundas are exhibited with multiple blooms on one stem. A group of florets

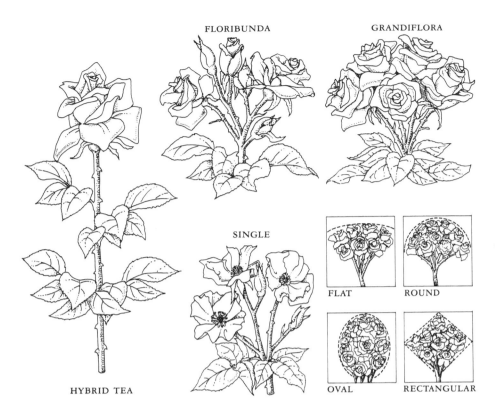

FLORIBUNDA   GRANDIFLORA

SINGLE

FLAT   ROUND

OVAL   RECTANGULAR

HYBRID TEA

VARIETY REQUIREMENTS
Hybrid teas *are most often exhibited one per stem. Form may be either exhibition or decorative, but the prissier varieties usually win blue ribbons.*

Floribundas are usually exhibited with multiple blooms on one stem. Blossoms should be at all stages of development— green buds as well as those at several stages of maturity.

Grandifloras are also exhibited as sprays as long as their masses of bloom are at the same stage of development. Judges know which varieties are capable of meeting this standard and the stages at which they best comply.

Single roses are those varieties with five to twelve petals surrounding a cluster of stamens. For singles, stamens take the place of centers, and their freshness is judged by the brightness of their colors.

Roses that bloom in sprays create an inflorescence with their blossoms. To win in competition, they may take any geometric form as long as they're pleasing to the judges' eyes.

on one stem constitutes a spray. The overall pattern the spray, or group of sprays, creates is called the inflorescence; it may be circular, oval, or any geometric form that pleases the eye.

The final consideration for ideal floribunda exhibition is stage of bloom. Ideally, inflorescences should show all stages of development: green buds; buds just beginning to open; blooms one-third, one-half, and three-quarter open; and blossoms fully open. With some varieties, stages of bloom are easily presented; they grow that way. With others, only two, or even one stage, appear at any given time on a spray of blooms. Since judges know that this characteristic is typical of the variety, these aren't overtly penalized, but a floribunda spray showing all stages of bloom will almost always win.

Grandifloras.   Often exhibited just like hybrid teas and judged exactly the same way, grandifloras have identical exhibition standards. When they have been exhibited one to a stem, winners can become eligible for yet higher awards: the Court of Honor.

When grandifloras are exhibited with multiple blooms on one stem, the judging criteria are the reverse of those for floribunda sprays. Here, all the blooms should be cut at the *same* stage of development, ideally classic exhibition form. They are then judged according to their individual flower form and their overall appearance.

Singles. Most rose shows include a division for single roses, those varieties with five to twelve petals and a cluster of stamens in the middle. For these varieties, stamens take the place of centers and weigh heavily in overall scoring. Stamens must be fresh, a quality best proved by their color, which should be bright, never faded. Stamen color differs by variety; judges know what is characteristic.

Court of Honor

Once the judging for specimens in a show has been completed, all judges participate in selecting the Court of Honor. The point of taking this collective vote, usually by secret written ballot, is to identify the best roses being shown. The highest award is for the Queen of the Show. Second is King, third is Princess. Some shows also add less-courtly ranks.

I shall never forget my first Queen of the Show. San Francisco's annual rose show is always on Mother's Day, the second Sunday in May. On the Friday before, I spotted a bloom of John F. Kennedy in my garden that was unlike any I had ever seen. It wasn't ready yet; it still had that greenish coloring this rose can have as it's maturing, before it becomes perfectly white. But it had all the makings of a winner.

Sure enough, on Sunday morning it had everything you'd want: a huge, stiff white bloom perched on top of an exemplary stem with abundant foliage. It needed practically no grooming at all, nor would you have needed any particular expertise to pick it as Queen if you had happened by the show. It set a new standard of excellence for me that day, and for some others as well, I suspect.

San Francisco takes Queens a step farther than most places. The annual rose show has an entry for Pair of Queens: two blooms of one variety displayed in a single bud vase. Rose varieties that have won Queen of the Show sometime during the previous ten years are eligible as entries.

I once entered the Pair of Queens competition with the blooms of Ernest H. Morse, a great turkey red rose with an unfortunate habit: it "blows" (opens fully) if it gets too warm. When I put my Ernests on the designated table, they were perfect and would have easily won a blue ribbon. Because of some show schedule mix-up, however, judges didn't consider any of the Queen pairs until the end of their alloted judging time. Alas, my pair of Queens had blown into dowagers, and I got a red (second place) ribbon while the blue went to a pair of Pascali that tightly held their form.

There may also be an award for the finest specimen exhibited, usually called Best in Show. Unlike the Queen, this rose needn't have classic, formal hybrid tea form. It may even be a single or a miniature, but it must be exemplary in what it has achieved for its variety.

Challenge Classes

Rose shows have challenge classes, which call for specific varieties or colors. Some specify that a hybrid tea, a floribunda, and a grandiflora be displayed together, or in separate containers. Another popular category is for the most fragrant rose in the show, judged by a sightless person. Yet another is for a dozen hybrid teas in one container (the effect of this is better than that of most arrangements). There are many challenge classes, but here are my favorite two.

Multiple Specimens.   This is the biggie. Whatever other challenges there are, this is the trophy hard-nosed competitors vie for.

Any number of specimen blooms may be required, from three to more than nine, but the big award is almost always for five or six, and occasionally for specific colors. Each specimen in an entry is displayed in a separate container, and a great deal of attention is given to how the roses are lined up to make the display as aesthetically pleasing as possible.

Usually, hybrid teas are called for, but sometimes grandifloras grown one to a stem are allowed as well. Overall size, balance, and proportion must be considered not only for each specimen, but for their combination. Obviously, the individual entries must complement each other; otherwise, the exhibit will lack cohesiveness and symmetry. All in all, this is the ultimate test for exhibition acumen.

English Box.   I recall well the first time I saw one of the exhibits in this challenge class. I thought it quite weird, and so might you. Here, all is bloom; there is no stem. The blossoms are arranged to fit into a box shape, with only a few inches of stem left, and none of it showing. Stems are immersed in water held in small vials under the holes cut into the open face of the box. Boxes of six to twenty-four blooms may be specified; six is usual for entries in American shows.

THE ENGLISH BOX
The British first thought of displaying prize rose blooms this way—flashy exhibition blossoms, with no stems in sight, inserted into water vials through the template of a rectangular box. Color and size combinations are important for winning, as is the overall visual impact of the exhibit.

Since no stem or foliage is seen, judging is for the bloom only. Again, the bigger and more form the better. Some shows call for blooms of only one variety in the English Box exhibits; most often, however, at least three varieties are specified. The exhibitor must carefully consider color and size combinations. As with other exhibits, an overall pleasing quality is the key.

Now after having seen many English Box exhibits, I have come to like them. I have a box in my house that I often fill and display on a coffee table. It's a great way of appreciating exhibition blooms, many of which never had a stem you wanted to look at anyway.

Bill Derveniotes, who staged the roses in this book for me to photograph, is about the best exhibitor I know. He has won scads of blue ribbons and trophies for English Box entries, one of his fortes. He'd like me to forget his first English Box entry, but I can't. I was clerking that particular day, so I heard all the inside poop.

Neither Bill nor I had many roses then, but for this show he did have bushes of Lady X and Medallion that were in full bloom. Lady X has never been one of my favorite roses. All by itself its pale mauve color looks funereal; with anything else it's ghastly. Medallion, on the other hand, is a wonderful light apricot. When he mentioned combining them for an English Box entry, I turned up my nose. He ignored me, knowing that I always sneered at anything having to do with Lady X.

When the judges arrived at the English Box entries, I got to hear everything they said, including one's asking another if the person who made that particular entry might be color-blind. If a black-and-white photograph taken of the entries had been used for judging, Bill would have won hands down. As it was, they gave him second place because the blooms were so well matched.

Grooming

Welcome to a world of artifice. Many roses, although infinitely capable of producing exhibition blooms, perversely insist on arriving at perfection too early or too late for show time. Thanks to certain techniques, however, they may be slowed down or hurried along.

If roses bloom a little too soon and aren't going to last, you can either refrigerate them or tie them with nonsticky corsage tape and leave them in a cool, dark place. If they're too tight and aren't going to open on the bush on time, you can cut them off and push moistened cotton wads down between their petals to hasten what nature would do in time. All grooming props must be removed before show time, of course, but their use can make all the difference.

Unsightly petal removal.   If you want to exhibit a rose, or if you just decide that the green or white streaks on its outside petals offend you, remove them. Don't be in such a hurry, however, that you pull at them and break them so they leave an unsightly stump. To take them off correctly, insert your thumb between the upper surface of the outside streaked petal and the under surface of the next petal row. While compressing the faulted petal against the crook of an index finger, rock it forward and backward until it snaps clean at its base. It may take several to-and-fro motions before the petal turns loose from a turgidly fresh specimen, but the result is worth the wait.

Cleaning foliage.   Cleaning rose leaves can have such a pleasing effect that you will want to try it whether or not you plan to exhibit. I've heard of all sorts of approaches. Some claim milk does wonders. I believe the idea is better than the result. Others use oil, tantamount to disqualification in exhibition, and otherwise just cosmetically offensive. My recommendation is clean water. Rinsing leaves of spray residue really does make a difference. If you care to go a step farther, even just to see what foliage groomed to a fare-thee-well looks like, try polishing cleaned and pat-dried leaves with a piece of velvet or old nylons.

Evidence of disease, particularly traces of mildew, can also be removed. If plain water doesn't do the trick, baking soda added to it surely will.

Brushing.   I have seen dowdy blooms become Queens in the hands of a good groomer with a camel-hair brush. Practically speaking, brushing is useful when you want a perfect bloom in the perfect bud vase and the bloom isn't quite ready. If properly stroked with a brush at strategic points near their bases, petals can be coaxed into almost anything.

If you really want to show off, try back-brushing the outer petals and making them curl and decoratively reflex. With thumb tip to base of petal, move the brush bristles in a circular motion *up* the petal's length. It's sort of like teasing hair, and gets petals ready for how you want to shape them.

Don't get carried away with what brushing can do for petal shap-

BRUSHING
A good exhibitor can make an ordinary rose look special with the help of a camel-hair water-color brush. When outer petals are back-brushed, they curl and reflex to the teaser's touch. Brushing can also speed up the maturity of the blooms that aren't quite ready to open.

ing. A bloom must be typical of its variety to win, and judges know what that is. If you make petals quill or reflex in a way that isn't natural to the variety, it doesn't matter how pretty it is, it won't win.

Label the roses you cut for a show before you leave home. I use a strip of plain paper looped loosely around stems and fastened by cutting a slit in one end and inserting the other end into it. Use a pencil or a waterproof pen for writing names; water will smear anything else. This may seem like a lot of trouble when you first do it, but you'll be happy when you can tell your Mon Cheri from your First Prize from your Color Magic from your Duet when you get to the show. If you misname roses, judges will not only disqualify them for awards, they'll write humiliating comments on your entry tag.

If you want to know more about exhibiting, and particularly if you are tempted to try it, you must read *Guidelines for Judging Roses*, a publication of the American Rose Society. You will learn a great deal more than the general suggestions presented here, and you will find information you *must* have regarding disqualification and penalization rules.

Arrangements

Three roses in a vase are about my limit. I don't believe roses *need* anything with them, and I tend to prefer them by themselves. I have stopped going into the arrangement section in rose shows because I never like what I see. While I concur that other foliage is sometimes appropriate, I don't like gimmicks such as plastic Madonnas, gilded leaves, or driftwood.

When I entered every category in rose shows for which I was eligible and found that I still had blooms to spare, I decided to try my hand at arranging. I was a flop in the eyes of the traditionalists, although once I did actually win a ribbon. The year Double Delight was introduced, 1977, I had four blooms of it on a rose show day. They had long passed exhibition stage and were dinner-plate size. I couldn't stand to leave them in the garden—they had to be seen to be believed.

I looked in the show schedule for arrangement themes and noted that there was one entitled Yesteryear. Just then the phone rang, and I went into the house. When I crossed the threshold to the kitchen, I noticed a plaster Victorian bracket that I was using as a doorstop. It sure looked "yesteryear" to me. I set it on end and found that one of my vases fit perfectly behind it, filling the space, but remaining concealed.

I cut the Double Delights and took them to the show along with the gingerbread remnant and my "real" entries. I really didn't arrange them at all. Some had become so top-heavy because of their enormous proportions that I just propped them up in a vase, and they arranged themselves.

I saw some noted arrangers look down their noses at my blue ribbon because my entry lacked a "focal point," but I'll bet if you asked someone at the show that day what they remembered from the arrangement section, they'd tell you about those huge red-and-white blooms.

I'm perfectly pleased with roses displayed rather than arranged, particularly at home. I like one specimen or a few blooms in bud vases placed all over the house.

Take lots of photographs of your prize-winning roses whether you exhibit them or not. You'll appreciate reminders of what roses look like when winter rains and temperatures call everything to a rude halt. Sharpen your shears and get ready to prune.

CHAPTER 8
Pruning

Nothing frightened me more when I started growing roses than pruning. I read up on the subject, went to demonstrations, and, still, when the time came, I stood with my shears and trembled in front of bushes that begged to be pruned. Cutting canes seemed so final, so noncorrectable. Now, on the other side, feeling comfortable, knowing exactly what I'm doing, I want to make it easy for you.

Why Prune?

Pruning is done for two reasons: (1) to eliminate older, nonproductive, or damaged wood, thereby encouraging new growth; and (2) to shape bushes.

Left to its own devices, a bush will become a tangled mess of small, insignificant flowers on weak, spindly stems. (Old wood left unpruned won't produce blooms at all.) And new growth for the coming season will be minimal without the stimulation pruning provides. All in all, there is no choice but to prune.

When to Prune

You will feel a strong urge to do something to rosebushes right after they have stopped blooming. Resist it. It is after they have done their work that they rest and collect their starches and sugars and go into dormancy. Without this period bushes can't store all they need. Where my bushes grow, roses never *really* go dormant; the climate is too mild. Even so, the process is similar and the resting time necessary.

For modern roses the pruning debate centers on winter versus spring pruning. Those in favor of winter pruning point out that bushes cut back early have a chance to adjust to their new shape and size, without supporting wood that's going to come off anyway. Those advocating later pruning point out that tender new growth can be brutally affected by late frosts and unseasonable cold spells. Listen to what Vita Sackville-West, an ardent rose grower herself, had to say about the subject:

> Argument still rages in the horticultural world about the best time of year to prune roses. According to the old orthodox theory, the time to do it was in the second half of March or in early April. Present-day opinion veers more and more strongly in favour of winter pruning. It seems to me common sense to cut the plant when it is dormant, rather than when the sap has begun to rise and must bleed the wound.
>
> I know there are objections. People say "Oh, but if you prune your roses in December or January, they may start to make fresh growth in the mild weather we sometimes get in February or early March, and then comes an iron frost and then what happens to those young tender shoots you have encouraged by your precipitate pruning?"
>
> All I can say in answer to that is that you will just have to go over your roses again and cut away all the frost-damaged shoots back to a new eye lower down the stem. You might have to do the same thing after a March pruning, so you will not have lost any time, and on the whole I am on the side of the winter pruners.

Of course, one must remember that Ms. Sackville-West was growing roses in England, where winters are severe. For most of us, controversial pruning months occur farther back in the calendar year. For instance, where I live, near the coast in northern California, there is argument whether to prune in December, January, or February, but all agree that pruning should be well over before March. In colder climates, pruning can be contemplated no sooner than late March.

I've experimented with both approaches. I've pruned half of the bushes of one variety early and the remainder some weeks later. They bloomed at about the same time. The only differences were the slightly longer stems and somewhat larger blooms produced by early pruning.

I now begin pruning the day after Christmas. First, I have some extra time then. Second, we never know how erratic the weather will be for the next two months. If the sun is shining, we prune. Besides, we have several thousand huge bushes staring us in the face and simply must begin as soon as we can.

My advice in sum: Prune as soon as possible once dormancy is safely broken, that is, when you're sure there won't be another hard freeze.

Ask your consulting rosarian for ideal pruning dates for where you live. County agricultural extensions usually have a suggestion, since all dormant plants, not just roses, need timely cutting back. Also, find out if there are any pruning demonstrations being given in your area. Many rose societies prune roses in their local municipal gardens and give informative lectures while they're doing it.

Stripping the Bush

You'll be very happy if you take this advice: Strip the bushes of *all* foliage two weeks before you prune. When leaves are removed from rosebushes, the plant is given a signal to rejuvenate the foliar process immediately.

The first sign the bush is bouncing back is when you spot swollen eyes where new growth is to appear—at the juncture of leaf formations and the stems on which they grow. When they are dormant, they may not be easily visible to the human eye. When their growth begins, however, accelerated by stripping, they swell, turn red, and become more obvious. When you arrive with pruning shears, you must find these landmarks in order to make cuts in the right places, so make it easy on yourself and give nature a chance to help you.

Foliage should be cut, not ripped, off. If you tear the leaves off, you may damage the bark just at the juncture where the dormant new bud eye is, stunting or preventing its development.

Dormant Spraying

Bushes stripped for pruning are ideal candidates for dormant sprays. These special spray materials are formulated to clean up any diseases a bush may be sheltering and provide a healthy environment for the coming new growth. They're quite safe and easy to use. There are many on the market, most with a base of sulfur, which is known for its effective disease eradication. If you plan to use a dormant spray, and I urge you to, please do it at this point. The spray is not meant for the new growth that will be appearing rapidly once you've stimulated the bush to provide it.

While you're at it, spray the soil around the bush as well. This area can harbor disease spores left from fallen leaves and cuttings, and dormant spray will safely knock them flat.

Tools

Pruning requires certain equipment without which you will injure yourself, the bush, or both.

First are gloves, preferably leather ones. Rose thorns are vicious, particularly at pruning time when dormancy has allowed them to harden and winter has whittled them sharp. You won't be able to make the necessary cuts without holding onto canes and thorny areas, so gloves are a must.

You will need shears, of course. Fortunately, you can use the same ones I recommended for maintenance and cutting. Just make sure they're sharp and remain so for as long as you prune. Cuts have to be clean, and stems must never be crushed or torn. Sharpen shears well before you begin, and again each time you feel them compromise a clean cut.

You can now buy shears that have a ratchet action. Progressive squeezes of the handle are made until the shears are tight enough to make an effortless cut. Pruning requires some hard squeezing, and ratchets may prove welcome after a short while.

If your bushes have been planted for more than one year, canes will have developed that are too thick to cut with shears, even ratchet-action ones. For those, you will need loppers or a saw. Loppers are those cutting tools with relatively small blades and handles twenty inches long. The extension of the arms provides the leverage needed for hard cuts. If canes you need to cut are in the way of each other, the only entries to the bud union may be small, requiring a narrow saw blade with which cuts flush with the bud union can be made. I have found that even with older bushes, I'm able to make 70 percent of my cuts with shears, and 20 percent with loppers. For the remaining 10 percent that hands, even in gloves, can't reach into, I must resort to a saw. Pruning saws designed specifically for these situations are ideal, and so are those saws called keyhole.

Shaping the Bush

It will help if you have a mental picture of what you are striving for in post-pruning shape. Ideally, modern rosebushes should form a classic urn shape, with canes radiating from the bud union, arching outward and upward around a free center. Opening the center of a bush is advised not only for appearance, but also for the more important reason that light must reach interior growth as part of the metabolic process for chlorophyll production. Also, a bush free of growth in its center has better interior air circulation, which helps prevent diseases such as mildew. Blooms appearing in the center of the bush are often wasted anyway, because they end up being deformed or badly damaged from rubbing against other unwanted growth.

Shaping bushes may not seem so important for you right at first.

It will become so as your bushes grow and mature. Many modern roses are vigorous growers, and they have to be kept within bounds if landscaping is a consideration. No matter what constraints you have, shaping at pruning time must be carried out with an eye toward the future, since you are creating the framework for all of next year's growth.

What to Take/Leave

Before you approach your rosebushes with a pair of shears, reacquaint yourself with terminology you learned in Chapter 4. As you know, rose wood comes in three sizes. Basal breaks, or main canes, are the largest and grow from the bud union. Laterals develop on canes, and stems grow on laterals.

First, take out what you *know* must come out: all twiggy growth, unhealthy wood or deadwood, and spindly tall growth that waves in the breeze at eye level, ready to poke you. Split bark is a sign of wood that probably must be removed. These openings, which are usually caused by stems rubbing against each other, are breeding grounds and entry spots for diseases.

Learn to judge the vigor of rose wood by examining the pith (inside wood) within bark. Creamy white or green, with no brown spots, is healthy. Brown or blackened wood is very old or dead and won't produce blooms. Fresh wood is much easier to cut than deadwood, and you'll learn to feel the difference with your shears.

Multiple canes coming from a single bud union will vary in color by age. New canes are often either quite red or a clean, healthy-looking green. Older wood is darker and more scaly. Some varieties make pruning easy for you by practically color coding their wood. Others produce wood of the same color, regardless of age, making pith examinations mandatory.

Don't confuse the age of rosebushes with the age of the canes that form them. Well-cared-for bushes may last for more than fifty years, and the bud union will become large and gnarled. New canes are produced each year. Canes are considered young for their first two years, then middle-aged for one year. Thereafter, they are old.

I have pruned bushes and removed every cane that wasn't produced that same year. I didn't set out to be tough—I just followed the bush's color-coded pruning guide.

Some beginners have found it helpful to identify those canes they

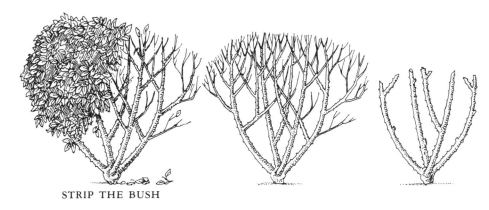

STRIP THE BUSH

HOW TO PRUNE A ROSE
Strip *the bush of all foliage, preferably two weeks before you approach it with shears. Bushes that are stripped of growth are given a signal to start over, resulting in swollen eyes where new growth will appear. These landmarks help eliminate pruning dilemmas.*

Remove all dead and twiggy growth *. Wood that has lived past its time won't rejuvenate, nor can growth develop that is thicker than the wood from which it grows. Since the goal of pruning is an urn-shaped rosebush with a free interior,* **remove canes that cross over the center** *of the bush.*

Cut remaining canes to the desired height *, depending on how severely you decide to prune. Make sure that each 45-degree cut is made one-quarter inch above a swelling bud that points away from the center of the bush.*

know they want to keep by clipping clothespins to them. If you do this, be sure not to damage any bud eyes when attaching clothespins. Above all, be sure to follow a cane with your eyes all the way up and down its length before you cut into it. Rose canes can be very deceptive in their crossing patterns, and you don't want to cut off a clothespinned cane.

Once only healthy wood is left, stand back to get an overall picture of the bush in order to decide how much more to take out. I like to leave at least four canes on any bush, and as many as ten on strong, proven growers and performers.

Experts suggest leaving three to six canes on bushes. Generally, these are the numbers you want to leave. But with vigorous, healthy growers, you would have a hard time deciding which six to leave. In fact, you should allow more to remain if the bush has proven that it can support them.

Pruning is one of those subjects for which there are no hard-and-fast rules, although generalities help. For instance, one usually leaves nothing on the bush except wood at least as thick as a pencil. For hybrid teas and grandifloras, this will usually be easy; not so for floribundas. These low-growing bushes produce stems that are more twiggy than larger bushes, but of wood that will support blooms.

Pruning for exhibition or simply for exhibition quality demands semicruelty. Stem length and size of bloom are important factors in exhibiting roses. To get what you need for a blue ribbon, you must prune severely.

If you grow roses for your own enjoyment, never plan to exhibit, and are pleased with something less than exhibition-quality blooms, you can afford to leave much more growth on bushes than those with

*How severely you prune your
bushes in winter will determine
how many blooms you have in
spring.* **Severe** *pruning (necessary in bitter winter climates)
results in fewer blossoms but
finer quality.* **Light** *pruning
will yield lots of showy garden
display, usually on flimsy
stems.* **Moderate** *pruning is a
compromise.*

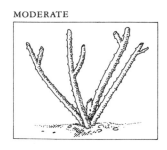

MODERATE

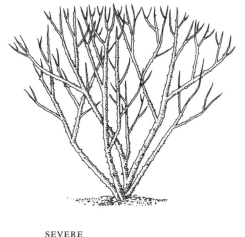

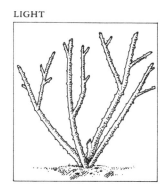

LIGHT

SEVERE

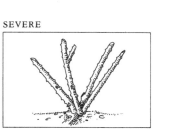

aspirations for showing. Stems probably won't be as long, or blossoms as large, but that may very well not matter to you. Form will
be affected very slightly—color and fragrance not at all.

Severity of pruning is dictated by either what you want the next
year's growth to be or by where you live. *Light* pruning requires a
minimum of cutting, with bushes left tall, after only twiggy and
obviously wrong wood or deadwood is removed. The goal is a profusion of short-stemmed blooms on a large bush. *Moderate* pruning
leaves five to ten, 1½- to 4-foot canes per bush, depending upon its
vigor and growth habits. Usually, half the length of each cane is
removed. There will be good garden display, and some exhibition
blooms, particularly from new, snapped basal breaks. *Severe* pruning
leaves only three to four canes, which are sometimes less than 1 foot
tall. In harsh winter climates severity may be necessary anyway for
winter protection. Exhibition freaks may do it for the showy yield.
It can be considered only for the most vigorous bushes; weak ones
can't take the shock.

I remember what it was like to see severe pruning tactics for the
first time. The rosarian who helped me conquer that particular fear
kept saying, "You have to take to get," as she ruthlessly hacked away.

Still, it takes time to become sufficiently heartless to do a thorough job. Often, it's necessary to remove sections larger than the bush was when it was planted. But look at it this way: a bush has only so much energy. Rather than diverting some of it to try to rejuvenate old wood that has produced all the good stuff it's likely to, why not remove it and hope that the energy it would have taken will be directed to new development in the form of basal breaks?

Ideal pruning height will vary by variety. Bushes don't grow the same or to a standard height, nor can they be pruned identically. Some grow tall, and nothing you do, including pruning them only inches from the ground, is going to make a difference finally. In fact, if you try to change some of their natural habits, they'll get back at you during the growing season by spending all of their time growing to the height at which they are comfortable for blooming. Until they get there, they may not bloom at all. Other tall bushes may have to be pruned severely, not because you would even consider changing their growth habits, but because if you don't, you won't be able to reach blooms without a ladder by summer's end.

People hate being told to use common sense, but pruning is a time when you simply must. If a bush has proven itself a hardy grower and bloomer, leave more than the usual number of canes. If there is a healthy new cane coming right from the center of the bush and crossing the middle of it, but it's the best you have to work with, leave it. If you have let a main cane develop above the height where a lateral should appear, cut into it. If a floribunda has performed for you on what looks like weak, spindly wood, treat it as if it's thicker than any pencil you've ever seen. If you have more than one bush of a variety, try pruning them differently to see for yourself what suits you best.

I've pruned bushes and left a cane that I wanted just for the first bloom. After the first flush, I cut it out just as I would have at pruning time. Remember that while major surgery is never performed during the growing season, lots can and should be taken out then. You can always take growth out later, but you can never graft it back.

Sometimes the best canes on a bush will be too close to each other, and you'll wish you could spread them apart. You can. Decide, within reason, how far apart you'd like to push them and cut a section that length from a cane you've already removed. Insert it into thorns on

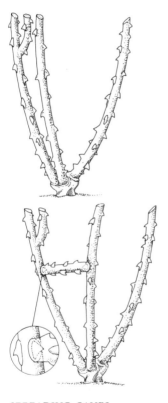

SPREADING CANES
The best canes on a rosebush are sometimes too close to each other. Rather than taking out one of them, spread them apart *with a length of rose wood from a cane that you've already cut off some bush. Thorns on the canes you want to spread will help to secure the temporary stretcher.*

the two canes you're separating. By midsummer the separation will be permanent and the prop can be removed. If you can't find it later because of the abundant foliage hiding it, just let it stay. No harm can be done, and the prop can safely remain until the canes themselves are eventually removed.

Your local consulting rosarian will prove invaluable yet again by letting you know about growth idiosyncracies in your area. I have visited growing areas where some varieties grow to twice the height of mine; others are lilliputian by comparison. In those cases it's not a question of superior growing conditions—it's purely locale.

I visited New Zealand recently and saw some wonderful roses. Some of the best were in the rose garden in Te Awamutu, a town of about 5,000 residents. So much was wonderful, but I'll always remember the Dainty Bess. When I first spotted it, I thought it was something else. It *looked* like Dainty Bess, but it was taller than any I had ever seen. Sure enough, it was, and they just grew it that much better than we. Just when I was starting to doubt our own growing culture, I spotted something that looked like Queen Elizabeth, but a floribunda version of our magnificent grandiflora. They just can't grow the Queen as well as we can (it's more Princess-like), so I got over the Dainty Bess one-upmanship. No rhyme or reason can explain this, you understand; we just all take what we get and push it to the limit.

Where to Cut

Dormant bud eyes will be readily apparent to you if you have stripped the bushes of foliage two weeks before pruning. Cuts are made a quarter inch above bud eyes, pointing outward from the center of the bush in the direction in which you want new growth to develop. Angles formed by cuts are ideally 45 degrees, with the downward slope toward the bush's center. Learn what a 45-degree cut looks like and eyeball your cuts.

Some experienced rosarians recommend never cutting into main canes; I am among them. The snapping procedure recommended in Chapter 4 was originally devised to avoid having to make cuts into main canes. Seeing what snapping new canes can do for bush development has persuaded me to recommend it for everyone. Once you do it, you won't have to worry about cutting into main canes; multiple laterals will develop from your snaps, and you can cut into those

RIGHT AND WRONG CUTS
Before you approach your rosebushes with shears, memorize the perfect pruning cut—the one on the left. Make your cuts on a 45-degree slope, about a quarter inch above a swelling bud eye. The cut in the middle is too flat and too far removed from its new eye; and the one on the right cuts too sharply into new growth.

laterals. If main canes are allowed to produce candelabra growth either because you didn't spot their development in time to snap them or because they came late in the growing season, you will have to cut into them. You have no choice, and it may very well not matter, especially if your bushes have been subjected to freezes.

Often a dormant eye pointing in the right direction is nowhere to be found. Do one of two things. One, make whatever cut you decide on higher than you'd like. This will allow for development of the bush and, more particularly, give time for buds to continue swelling and become apparent. Later, when they are apparent, you cut to the right one. Two, make cuts that leave quarter-inch stubs of old stems. Dormant eyes abound just under the junctures of stems and what they grow on. You will leave a "knobby" end to a cane or lateral by making these cuts, but growth coming from them will disguise it soon enough. It looks strange when you first do it, and not as clean or ideal as a cut above a bud eye, but it really will work.

At the Bud Union

When whole canes have to be removed, they must be cut at the bud union. Rosarians disagree about exactly how these cuts should be made. Some say the cut should be as flush to the surface as possible. Others recommend leaving a quarter-inch stub that can harbor dormant eyes for future basal breaks. If I err here, it will be on the side of caution. Nothing is lost by leaving a cleanly cut quarter-inch stub. The bud union can still be shapely, and if new growth is really waiting there, I want it.

If, as a beginning pruner, you're in doubt about some wood on a bush, leave it. Try to remember to watch what you reluctantly left and see what happens. If it turns out to have been a mistake, take it out later. As you gain experience, the recommended approach will be exactly the opposite: if you have any doubt about wood's worth, take it out.

After Pruning

Should you seal pruning cuts? Recommended pruning sealants include orange shellac, rose paste, tree-wound paint, and aerosol sprays. I used these concoctions the first two years I pruned seriously. Later I learned that sealing was just so much busywork, since it's really meant for those who must protect against caneborers, and those pests aren't found in my area. Check to see if you have any such pests or if your local consulting rosarian knows of any other regional peculiarity that might require sealing.

As for sealing pruning "wounds," that shouldn't be necessary if you prune at the right time. If sealing is required in your area, you might at least restrict your efforts to those cuts larger than one-half inch in diameter.

Cleaning up after pruning is another matter. Everyone must do it. All foliage, twigs, and cuttings should be removed from bush areas; they just lead to disease.

After you prune, settle back in your easy chair and read the catalogues that have begun arriving; they'll tempt you. So will I with my twenty-four best bets.

CHAPTER 9
Great Modern Roses

Two Dozen Best Bets

First I should declare the biases that dictated these selections. I think roses should be fragrant. Other admirable qualities have to be tremendous to make up for lack of scent. I also prefer large blooms to small, and blossoms that reach the fully open stage to those that stop short of it. Finally, I like *lots* of blooms at regular, short intervals from spring through fall.

With those biases in mind, here is my list of two dozen readily available, surefire winners. Order is by color, *not* preference. All varieties have been ranked 8.0 or higher by voting members of the American Rose Society. As mentioned in Chapter 2, scores between 8.0 and 8.9 are given roses deemed "excellent." Scores from 9.0 to 9.9 are those called "outstanding," a rating not issued casually, since only five modern roses, excluding miniatures, carry it at the time of this writing. The perfect 10.0 has yet to be awarded.

Following the name of each variety, you will see its heritage. The female parent is always listed first. Sometimes there is multiple parentage. Occasionally, a parent will be labeled "unknown." I may be giving you more information than you need at this point, but your thirst for these facts will grow as your interest grows. You may learn that you like a variety so much that you also want its child. Or you may get so fed up with something that you want nothing more to do with it or its progeny.

I've selected the photographs for the twenty-four varieties according to my idea of their best stages of bloom. For most, this occurs somewhere between the half and three-quarter stage. A few are outstanding in bud, some when fully blown.

Mister Lincoln
Chrysler Imperial x Charles Mallerin

The great American hybridizing duo of Swim and Weeks crossed Chrysler Imperial and Charles Mallerin to get two wonderful, dark red seedlings for introduction in 1964. One was Mister Lincoln, the other Oklahoma. Meilland of France produced Papa Meilland the preceding year from the *same* parentage.

In 1965 Mister Lincoln won an All-America award. It has since earned a 9.1 rating and has become the favorite dark red rose of the majority of rosarians in the world. This hardy, robust rose is long on fragrance.

Mister Lincoln should always be grown one to a stem. Fortunately, that is easy to do, since new growth needs disbudding less often than most hybrid teas.

While both Oklahoma and Papa Meilland are similar to Mister Lincoln in that they are also dark red (even darker) and intensely fragrant, Mister Lincoln outdoes them primarily because the bush is a prolific bloomer. It has a nice habit of growing upright and can be readily pruned to the classic urn shape.

I can't count the people who have asked me if I've seen the "black rose," then argue when I claim it doesn't exist. Mister Lincoln is as black as I care a red rose to be while it's in bud. As it opens, the center petalage proves to be a much lighter, cherry red, and it's intensely fragrant all the while. The blooms appear with satisfying regularity, with a quick repeat bloom cycle. Admittedly, Mister Lincoln has a tendency to "blue" toward the end of its very long vase life. But let's give it a break. No one has yet produced a perfect 10.0.

Fragrant Cloud
Unknown seedling x Prima Ballerina

Tantau of West Germany has hybridized some terrific roses, but his best in my book came in 1963. Fragrant Cloud didn't make it to the United States until 1968, and has been a favorite ever since. In Europe it is also known as Duftwolke and Nuage Parfumé.

Here's a hybrid tea to silence those critics of modern roses who complain about lack of scent. Stick their noses into some of these blooms; the fragrance is ravishing.

Although it has only twenty-five to thirty petals, the bloom is exceptionally well formed. Its official color classification is orange-red (I think of it as lipstick red), a color I've found no one ambivalent about. You either love it or hate it. Not a soul, however, will quarrel with the fragrance, and it boasts a host of international awards for that very quality.

Fragrant Cloud should be disbudded for true hybrid tea blooms of one to a stem. It *will* produce sprays if this strikes your fancy, but for this variety, I don't find multiple blooms on one stem desirable. The color is not one that mixes well, except with white. I prefer it all by itself in bud vases. As the bloom ages, it can take on a silvery cast that many find appealing. (It looks awful under fluorescent light, however.)

Blossoms of this cultivar have a persistent fault that will probably concern you only if you plant to exhibit. One or two, no more than three, outer petals have a greenish white streak through the middle. As the bloom opens, you won't notice them since the outer petals fold back and conceal the color difference.

The streaks don't bother me, and unless I plan to exhibit, I leave them. They are a fault in exhibition and cost points. In that case, or if they bother you, remove them as instructed in Chapter 8.

Precious Platinum
Red Planet x Franklin Engelmann

If you had asked me which rose variety I was most worried about when we planted our first bushes at Garden Valley Ranch, Precious Platinum would have been my ready answer. The bushes were puny compared to everything else we planted. Our Precious Platinums are now among the most vigorous growers in the field and must be pruned ruthlessly just to keep them within bounds. Blooms will appear in profusion almost whether you prune or not, but the bush will take over if you're not careful.

For all its robustness as a grower, Precious Platinum's bushes produce some of the classiest hybrid tea red roses there are. What's more, the fragrance is long on classic tea flavor. Blooms have two other distinctions: they're stiffly substantial and they get prettier as they open. In fact, I'm not fond of Precious Platinum in bud. Until blooms reach at least the quarter-open stage, they're mostly matte black and reveal little of the bright, clear red that is to come. As buds begin to open, their true color is revealed.

When Precious Platinum blooms reach the half-open stage, it's,

Katie, bar the door. If you yearn for huge, fragrant red roses, this one's for you. Don't worry about how big blooms become—when you go to cut them, you'll find proportionate stem and foliage. I like everything Precious Platinum does from the half-open to the fully blown stage. Color won't fade, and substance is held even in the petals that eventually drop.

Dickson of England has declared a hybridizing platform to develop the perfect red rose. He has given us some great ones, such as Red Devil and Portland Trailblazer (Big Chief in Europe), but Precious Platinum gets my vote for his best effort so far.

Precious Platinum is one of those roses that may perform better in one season than another. For us the best blossoms come in early fall. Spring bloom is nice, but September works magic.

Europeana
Ruth Leuwerik x Rosemary Rose

Why it took Europeana five years to reach American shores after de Ruiter of Holland hybridized it in 1963, I'm not quite sure. It was an All-America Selection for 1968 and has since endeared itself with two characteristics that will keep it in the floribunda foreground for a long time to come. First, its color. There are lots of reds, but not enough rubies. Europeana is a dark red that holds its color from start to finish. Second, Europeana is the most exemplary floribunda I know for geometric inflorescences of multiple blooms on one stem, rather than blossoms placed randomly here and there. Europeana read the show rules and took them to heart. You still have to remove the terminal bud, but once you do, sit back in confident anticipation of a great spray of bloom.

I must admit that I didn't like Europeana when I first saw it. Rosette-shaped blooms weren't what I was looking for. Now Europeana has grown on me, and I see why it's such a great rose. Fragrance is light but definite.

If the color and size work for you, Europeana is a terrific landscape rose. It's low-growing, almost as wide as tall, and clothed in glossy dark green foliage that retains strong hints of mahogany.

Europeana has dominated the exhibition floribunda class for more than a decade, but a rival is making its way up through the ranks—Showbiz, a bright red floribunda that was the only All-America Selection for 1985. When I first heard about Showbiz, rumor had it that it would push Europeana off the show table. It's too soon to know what will happen in exhibition since Showbiz has only recently been entered in competition, but my money's on Europeana.

Duet

Fandango x Roundelay

Once, for lack of something better to do, I kept count of every rose produced on every bush in my private San Francisco garden. Duet was the hands-down winner.

You'd expect a workhorse to be some other color, but here it is, producing scads of medium pink blooms with a darker pink reverse. What's more, blooms last and will open fully from bud, on the bush, or in a vase. Fragrance isn't strong, but it's there.

Duet is classified as a hybrid tea, as it should be, but it was first introduced as a grandiflora because of its tendency to produce multiple blooms on one stem. It needs disbudding. Foliage develops into a dark, glossy green, but when it first appears, it may have a funny habit about which you should be warned. While foliage of most varieties starts out fairly flat, Duet's is sometimes curly. Simply leave it alone, and it will flatten. The bush is hardly exemplary in its growth habit; instead of the desired urn shape, growth is very zigzag. Proper pruning can correct a lot, and no matter what you do, blooms will follow.

Sometimes when blooms are mature and you cut them from the bush, you notice that there are large gaps in foliage. What's more, leaves can be whimsically attached to their stems. If you're exhibiting, you can twist the foliage around and it will eventually behave. If you're arranging, you won't notice the difference because you'll have so many stems that their collective foliage will mass nicely.

How does a workhorse perform at the show table? Duet isn't famed for its exhibition value, but I've won Queen of the Show with it. What's more, it made the King (second place) look like a commoner.

Duet was an All-America Selection in 1961 and has been a rosarian's rose ever since. If you plant a bush of it, you'll join the fan club.

Dainty Bess

Ophelia x K. of K.

Back when I first admitted an interest in growing roses, I declared that there would be no pinks or singles in my garden. I was told that in time I'd come around to singles, but that I had to get over my aversion to pinks right away—more great roses are pink or blends thereof than any other color. I've now come full circle. Here is a pink single I wouldn't want to do without.

The reason I paid little attention to single varieties at first was that I thought they were not fragrant or long-lived. I was wrong on both counts. Many single roses are strongly scented and have as long a vase life as any of the more heavily petaled varieties. Dainty Bess is certainly one of those, and even when cut in tight bud it will unfurl itself in a vase.

Dainty Bess has been the most popular and acclaimed single hybrid tea for sixty years. It has only five petals, but they're broad and fragrant. They also completely surround a center of maroon stamens. Maroon might not seem like a big deal if you don't know that 90 percent of stamens are yellow. I think Dainty Bess would be a winner if its stamens *were* yellow. Maroon makes it a shoo-in.

Most people describe the bloom as dusky pink. That's one of the shades, but there are more, depending on where the bloom appears on the bush and how much sun it's exposed to. Blossoms close at night.

The bloom is so fragile-looking that you expect a tender bush to go with it. Dainty Bess is quite the opposite, with an upright, tall, prolific plant clothed in tough foliage.

I wish my Dainty Bess were as tall as those I've seen in New Zealand and Australia. My bushes don't grow higher than four feet no matter what I do, but their long-stemmed blooms are second to no other single.

Aquarius
(Charlotte Armstrong x Contrast)
x
{Fandango x (World's Fair x Floradora)}

The only reason Aquarius isn't considered even greater than it is, in spite of its horribly complicated parentage, is that it's in such a tough color class; pinks are abundant. Aquarius does have some extras going for it though; it's outstanding in sprays or one to a stem, and the color is downright incredible. When you look down into a good bloom, it seems as though a tiny artificial light has been inserted into its base—it fairly glows shades of pink with an ever-so-slight hint of lavender.

Aquarius is an outstanding grandiflora. It's prolific, almost naturally urn shaped as a bush, and covered in thick disease-resistant foliage. It was an All-America Selection in 1971.

Blooms begin with buds a dark pink blend and fully open as light pink blossoms. And they last. Once I took a dozen to an Aquarian friend of mine on the 4th of July. I told him that I could never have them on his birthday (January 31), so this was my premature gift. I took them in tight bud, knowing they would open fully because of the conditioning I had given them. I had to restrain myself from calling to learn what happened, though I later heard they opened.

If you can't decide how to approach disbudding, Aquarius is the rose for you. It's wonderful one to a stem, in sprays, or both on the same bush. If only two or three buds form at the end of a stem, I leave the terminal bud and remove the smaller ones. If four or more buds form, I remove only the terminal bud. Since the blooms of Aquarius are a bit too small to suit me, I like sprays where overall size make up for smaller-than-average individual blooms.

Queen Elizabeth
Charlotte Armstrong x Floradora

Queen Elizabeth was the very first grandiflora. It was created by the great American hybridizer Walter Lammerts in 1954 and was the All-America Selection for 1955. It was voted the world's favorite rose in 1978 by the World Federation of Rose Societies. Thirty years after its introduction, it's the number-one exhibition rose of the grandiflora class.

Queen Elizabeth's numerous plaudits are well deserved since it is indeed a regal bush and bloom. The Queen is a very tall grower. Don't try to coerce her into shorter height by pruning too low, or she will spend most of the growing season reaching the height at which she blooms comfortably. After growing for two years, my bushes are 8 to 9 feet tall when I face them for pruning, and I reduce them to a minimum of 4 to 4½ feet.

If you have height limitations in your landscape, plant something else. If you can respect its lofty habits, Queen Elizabeth will reward you with panicles of rose and dawn pink blooms of thirty-seven to forty petals each, occurring mostly in clusters. Disbudding should be geared toward producing these multiple blooms on one stem. The bush will produce single blooms no matter what you do, and they're pretty, but the sprays are more impressive, and once bushes are established, you can easily cut inflorescences with two-to-three-foot stems. The foliage is large, dark, glossy, and leathery.

Besides its stately bush, Queen Elizabeth's disease-resistance is a great plus, as is its vigor. Wini Edmunds says in her catalogue: "They can be grown by anyone who can make weeds thrive." She's right, and the benefits are ever so much more rewarding.

The 9.1 rating by the ARS is no accident; it has been reviewed regularly for thirty years. I think it will be some time before the Queen is dethroned, although Gold Medal is in hot pursuit of the number-one exhibition grandiflora spot.

Cherish

Bridal Pink x Matador

When this rose was being tested for All-America Selection, I heard an expert (who should have known better) call Cherish "just another pink floribunda." Boy, was he wrong!

America's Bill Warriner made a clean sweep of the All-America Rose Selections in 1980. Love, a red-and-white bicolor grandiflora, and Honor, a white hybrid tea, were chosen along with Cherish. I never took Love seriously; its growth habit is weak and erratic, and the blooms too often lack form. I like Honor, though not as much as other whites. Cherish is another matter. First of all, in spite of its low-growing characteristics, Cherish is a producer. The blooms are a wonderful clear pink, with high-centered hybrid tea form. They do occur singly, especially early in the season, but they're best in sprays.

Cherish's foliage is disease-resistant and large for a floribunda. Leaves are a dark matte green with a mahogany overlay. The bushes tend to spread, but this is easily corrected at pruning time for good shape (though they'll always be low to the ground). Blooms become very large before they open fully, and their vase life is impressive.

I went with Bill Derveniotes, the exhibitor who groomed some of the roses for the photographs in this chapter, to help him compete in the National Rose Convention in Nashville, Tennessee, in 1982. We took along some blooms of Cherish to enter in a floribunda spray competition. When fellow exhibitors mentioned how lucky we were to have sprays of Cherish, I didn't understand what they meant; we always have them in sprays. Apparently, others don't. However Cherish chooses to present itself, you'll love the blooms.

You'll recall an ideal floribunda virtue is a presentation of all stages of bloom in one spray. Cherish doesn't seem to know how to spray any other way, making it a formidable opponent at the show table.

Royal Highness
Virgo x Peace

If you've been paying attention, you're aware that I don't much care for roses in bud. Here's the exception. There's no more elegant bud in all of rosedom than that of Royal Highness. It's frosty pink (about as light as it could be and still be classified as pink) and was the first hybrid tea of this color to be selected as All-America. It was chosen in 1963 and has reigned ever since.

Royal Highness has a number of appealing qualities, starting with an affinity for one-to-a-stem growth. Stems are long and cloaked in dark green foliage. Although the open bloom of Royal Highness can be a little loose, verging on blowsy, it's always pretty. Fragrance is light, but somehow fitting for this color.

The bush is about as classic as the bud. It's tall, upright, and almost naturally urn shaped, making pruning easy.

When I first grew this rose, I didn't understand the importance of spraying and I didn't regularly apply what I did know. It seemed improbable that mildew should attack something that looked so impenetrable. But it did, and it wasn't a pretty sight. Even so, it's more disease-resistant than most of the roses in this color range. I didn't include Royal Highness when Garden Valley Ranch was first planted because I shied away from mildewers. Now that I've learned to control the fungus, we have lots of Royal Highness bushes.

There's more good and bad news when it comes to maintaining Royal Highness. It doesn't rainspot as much as most roses, but it will rust in a flash if you don't spray preventively.

Royal Highness is yet another winner from the American hybridizing team of Swim and Weeks. Although it has lost its patent, Royal Highness will stay around until something worthy takes its place—a day not yet in clear sight.

Simplicity
Iceberg x Unnamed seedling

Some years ago, when the cost of fencing materials escalated, as did other building supplies, someone figured out that rosebushes might make comparatively inexpensive barricades. Armstrong Nurseries was the first to introduce the "living fence" concept. Its choice of rosebushes was an unfortunate one—Confetti, a garish blend of red, orange, and yellow that just doesn't work unless your intent is to make a bold, harsh statement.

Jackson & Perkins carried the idea to tasteful fruition when their hybridizer Bill Warriner rose to the occasion with a good bush that produces scades of pretty blooms. Simplicity, unlike Confetti, is of a color that's easy to live with. Shell pink to midpink wears well on the eyes.

The bush lends itself nicely to being trained as a hedge. Growth is compact and columnar, with foliage equally projected everywhere along its height, from base to tip.

Sprays of blossoms should be encouraged since one-to-a-stem blooms are really too small to amount to much. Clustered on a stem, however, they're downright impressive, and they bloom in exemplary floribunda fashion, with all stages occurring at one time. Stems are relatively thin, but obviously draw water well since Simplicity's vase life is considered "extended."

There are only eighteen to twenty petals per bloom, so you'll often see stamens in fully open blossoms while you're still enjoying buds to blooms three-quarters open. The nice part about fully open blossoms is that their stamens are bright yellow and dense.

Foliage is proportionately small and olive green. Fragrance is light, but fresh. If you should decide to plant Simplicity as a living fence, you'll never be without roses for the house during its long blooming season.

Pascali
Queen Elizabeth x White Butterfly

I have a friend who has only white flowers in his garden. Half of them are roses, and they're almost all Pascali. It's *the* white rose if you want purity with no shadings of color.

Hybridized by Lens in 1963, this is the only rose of international importance from Belgium. The name is synonymous with Easter, and the rose was selected as All-America in 1969. Where it grows well, it performs wonderfully.

Pascali will keep your disbudding fingers busy since it doesn't seem to know that it's prettiest one to a stem. Blooms are pure white with stiffly perfect form.

Often when I cut a bloom of Pascali, I complain that it's too small. Some days later (when it has actually grown in its vase) I take back what I said. The blooms almost always have classic form, rarely with split centers.

When you compare this bush with other hybrid teas, the stems appear weak and unable to support a large bloom, even one with only thirty petals. But they're strong and prove to be more supportive than larger, thicker stems. Then, too, the diameter of the stems must lend itself well to drawing water, since blooms last amazingly well. The ARS rating of 8.7 is well deserved, and Pascali is still among the ten most highly rated exhibition roses in the United States.

Of all the white hybrid teas we grow, Pascali is probably the most popular with florists. They don't always realize that the reason they like the foliage is that Pascali is so disease-resistant. They know well, however, that Pascali is a superb cut flower and it has an unusually extended vase life.

Pristine
White Masterpiece x First Prize

Pristine, a pinkish white bloom that looks like porcelain, caused quite a commotion when it was introduced in 1978. Another result of Bill Warriner's hybridizing efforts for Jackson & Perkins, Pristine quickly climbed to the top of the chart of great exhibition roses, where it is likely to remain. It gets my vote for the rose of the seventies.

The bush and the bloom are unusual in combination because few plants growing this hardily produce blossoms of such delicate color and form. Bushes look as if they would resist anything from disease to bodily interference. Pristine is a rampant grower and sends up large numbers of thorny, tough canes. It can grow very tall if you let it, but it will also respond to controlled shaping. The foliage is large and tough and starts out as waxy, mahogany red, turning dark green as the bloom matures. New canes are also dark red and obviously bursting with vigor from the number of stems swelling out all along their length. The arrangement of twenty-five to thirty large petals is unique for modern hybrid teas. It actually resembles a gardenia bloom. The petal edges are a pronounced lavender–rose pink.

Usually blooms in this color class are fragile and ephemeral. Not Pristine. Blooms last, and petals always have sufficient substance to present nice form. The fragrance is less than we might like, but that's the single flaw I find. Whites are not known for their fragrance, and Pristine actually has more than most. Stems are very long, and if you remove their vicious thorns, one long-stemmed bloom makes a wonderful "bouquet" for a bride to carry down the aisle.

Disbudding isn't needed very often, but side buds should be removed to get full hybrid tea beauty. I must admit, however, that I've seen sprays of Pristine that would knock your socks off.

Iceberg
Robin Hood x Virgo

The Kordes clan of Holstein, West Germany, has made countless contributions to the world of roses. Their hybridizing efforts have been so prodigious that they developed an entirely new botanical species of roses along the way. It seems odd that perhaps the finest Kordes effort came so early—in 1958 when they introduced Schneewittchen, now better known as Iceberg. The prestigious World Federation of Rose Societies picked Iceberg as the only floribunda among the federation's five favorite roses selected to date.

Iceberg blossoms are pure white and almost always appear in sprays. Petal count is low, so there are often fully open blooms to look at while sprays are still fresh. Fragrance is moderately strong and clean. Foliage is light green, small, and glossy. (It's also particularly prone to mildew.)

Iceberg makes a fine bush for landscaping, since it will do almost anything you want it to. With moderately severe pruning, bushes will remain compact and low enough for foreground plantings. Pruned for garden display, plants will easily oblige with growth sufficient for backgrounds.

Disbudding seems like a special chore, for bushes produce so many sprays, and all, it seems, at the same time. But your efforts will pay off with masses of icy white sprays that last well on or off the bush.

Someone recently asked a panel of rose breeders to name their favorite rose. Most of the experts couldn't see beyond their own hybridizing palettes and seized the opportunity to laud roses they had created themselves. Not Sam McGredy of the famous Irish rose dynasty. He dodged the question at first by saying that he wished he'd been asked to name the *best* rose in the world. "That would be easy—Iceberg."

GRANADA, PAGE 131

PASCALI, PAGE 110   JUST JOEY, PAGE 142

WHITE LIGHTNIN', PAGE 141

PARADISE, PAGE 134

GOLD MEDAL, PAGE 136

PRISTINE, PAGE 111

NATIONAL TRUST, PAGE 141

PEACE, PAGE 135   FIRST PRIZE, PAGE 130

DAINTY BESS, PAGE 105

MISTER LINCOLN, PAGE 102

BRANDY, PAGE 141

Color Magic
Unnamed seedling x Spellbinder

If you want to make rosarians really squirm, ask them to name their favorite rose. They can rattle off their favorite ten, but coming down to one is pretty tough. Some years ago, I decided that I had to pick my favorite so that I could give a shorter answer to that popular question. Color Magic is my choice. It meets my three chief requirements: blooms are large and irresistibly fragrant, with a scent, I believe, all its own, and it *can* be prolific.

When Bill Warriner introduced Spellbinder in 1975, I knew he was on to something great. Three years later, he crossed Spellbinder with an unknown seedling and got Color Magic. He won an All-America Selection for that particular effort.

The bloom's basic color is apricot pink, but this hybrid tea is truly a blend, with colors ranging from dark rose pink all the way to a rich, buff beige center. The size is simply staggering, and the more blooms open, the more beautiful they become. Fully open ones will easily fill a nine-inch space, and the exhibition stage between half and three-quarters open is something to behold.

I think I can identify Color Magic fragrance blindfolded. It has that quality some call classic tea scent, but it's strong and full-bodied. Stems are long and large, and if you can grow the bush well, you must treat it harshly to keep gargantuan growth from developing.

What keeps this variety from earning a 10.0 in my book is its propensity to die back (as discussed in Chapter 4), more so than any rose I know. Often at pruning time, after the dieback is cut off, there aren't enough canes left to justify leaving the bush in the ground. I'm getting somewhat better at handling the problem by cutting dieback off as soon as I spot it, and I certainly haven't given up because once I produce a good bloom, I remember that no other rose I know can beat it.

Double Delight
Granada x Garden Party

I saw a photograph of this rose before seeing the bloom itself and was sure that the suppliers were playing a trick on us. Double Delight is indeed something else. Blooms really are red and white, and the colors are dramatically combined. Red sprawls irregularly over the white petals. Sun and variable weather conditions produce different color patterns so that no two blooms are ever exactly alike. Add to this a strong fragrance and great form, and it's clear why Double Delight is so popular. It was selected as an All-America Rose for 1977 and quickly zoomed into the top ten of exhibition roses.

The bush is strong and produces an amazing number of blooms. All degrees of openness are nice, but the exhibition stage is best. It is also perfectly wonderful when fully open, and the colors remain strong, as does the spicy fragrance. Medium green foliage is abundant, but not particularly notable.

Double Delight is considered to be moderately disease-resistant. That it's not covered in mildew all the time is a wonder, considering its heritage. Its parents, Granada and Garden Party, set standards for mildew in most large rose gardens.

Three years after its introduction, Double Delight produced an offspring, Mon Cheri, which, although not quite as impressive as its parent, is also a wonderful rose, particularly if you prefer pink rather than white combined with red. It, too, is fragrant, large, and produced in large quantities on a bush quite similar to its predecessor.

Armstrong Nurseries has recently introduced a climbing version of Double Delight for those of you who might want to splash your garden walls or a trellis with red and white.

First Prize

Enchantment seedling x Golden Masterpiece seedling

There was only one All-America Rose Selection in 1970, probably because nothing else could stand up to hybridizer Boerner's First Prize to share the honors. Once First Prize was introduced, it cut a beeline for the number-one spot in the list of exhibition roses.

First Prize is a fabulous rose for lots of reasons, one being its fantastic blend of colors. It starts out as a high-centered pink, but with deep pink outer petals. Before it has finished opening, beige becomes the center's major color. Blooms reach amazing proportions with only twenty-five petals, probably because not a single one is misplaced in the creation of classic hybrid tea form.

The bush of First Prize is deceptive. It looks as though it's doing all the right things until you go to cut blooms and find too many with short stems. If you catch new basal breaks in time to snap them, you'll be rewarded with some long stems.

For those who have to consider what freezing weather might do, I'm told that the bush is winter tender. I can attest to its tendency toward mildew in spite of apparent vigor. When it produces blooms the size of dinner plates, though, it's easy to forgive all the faults.

For the first few years I grew First Prize, I thought it scentless; then one day I got a hint of its perfume. Other people I know still detect no fragrance. If you're after strong scent, don't plant First Prize. If you think you might someday like to exhibit, don't think of doing without it.

Competition can be toughest when it's between family members. In 1978 First Prize fathered Pristine, which has given it a run for its money. Father and child are likely to fight for the number-one spot in rose showiness for some time to come.

Granada
Tiffany x Cavalcade

Hybridized by Lindquist in 1963 and an All-America Selection in 1964, this hybrid tea is as popular twenty years later as it was when it was introduced. It strongly complies with two of my requirements in that it is a prolific bloomer and intensely fragrant. My quarrel is with its size; it's smaller than I would like. But the blooms come regularly and in abundance. Many call it the "birthday cake rose" because it looks so like the confection roses used with icings to decorate baked goods.

Its most impressive colors include vermilion, scarlet, and lemon yellow, the combination of which yields an eye-blinking fluorescent quality. The buds are urn shaped and can be cut tight; they'll still open, and the colors will intensify.

The bush of Granada can be identified even without blooms to help. Plants are low to medium height and clothed in somewhat crinkled foliage that is distinctly toothed. Often, another distinguishing characteristic is a set of highly decorative sepals, which can be amazingly long, elegantly framing the blooms. Unfortunately, the bush tends to be a bit tender and prone to mildew. All in all, however, it's a fine rose, and many consider it one of the most fragrant of modern introductions.

Granada has another endearing characteristic: it has always been the first rose in my garden to bloom. Understand that when roses finally bloom in spring, weeks after you wish they had, the first bloom is a welcome sight. Granada used to be the last to bloom for me as well. Now Gold Medal has that particular honor. But there is rarely a time when I can't find *some* Granada to cut, and that's a comfort when I take my shears to the garden knowing I must return with some roses.

Sea Pearl
Kordes' Perfecta x Montezuma

When Dickson of England introduced this unique floribunda, he didn't choose its name casually; it grows and blooms best in coastal climates. There it defies the generality that floribundas are low growing. (Actually, I think it's misclassed by the ARS—it should be a grandiflora.) Where I grow it, the bushes are taller than any other floribunda in sight, and reach a greater height than most of the hybrid teas as well. And it will do you no good to try to change its tall growth habit with severe pruning. It will bloom more quickly if you prune it tall.

The basic color of the bloom is peach pink, diffused with a buff-and-yellow reverse. There are only about twenty-two petals, but they're used to full advantage the way they form the bloom. If buds are cut tight, blooms will open fully and reveal golden stamens.

You can hardly believe that the blooms cut in the fall have come from the same bush as those you cut in spring. Colors remain the same, but they shade darker. It's hard to decide which is prettier. Fragrance is there from start to finish. Florists commonly refer to the lasting quality of flowers as vase life. Sea Pearl has it in spades.

While its growing habits are not typical of the floribunda class, Sea Pearl's blooming characteristics are ideal. More often than not, blooms are produced in sprays rather than one to a stem. And they must be disbudded if you are to enjoy them at their best. In competition, disbudding is mandatory. Once you understand what this maintenance technique can do for you, you'll disbud religiously.

Sea Pearl grows upright with wonderful urn-shaped, many-caned bushes. Some general pruning methods have to be ignored for this variety.

Grown well, the bushes are so hardy that they will support many more canes than most rosebushes. The foliage is not particularly distinguished, but it is a nice dark green and generally much healthier than most.

Anabell
Zorina x Colour Wonder

I'm not particularly fond of orange as a color for roses, but those who like it are a lucky lot, for there are some impressive orange roses around. Most come from Europe, more particularly, from the hybridizing efforts of the Kordes family in West Germany, who seem to have the corner on the orange market. An interesting note is that a parent for many of the orange varieties is frequently an older rose named Colour Wonder. I find Colour Wonder downright ugly—not because it's orange, but because of its dumpy formlessness. It's a great example of how complicated the results of hybridizing can be. While even orange enthusiasts wouldn't want a garden full of Colour Wonder, the rose makes a great parent (either sex).

As far as I'm concerned, two other orange roses from Kordes are worth considering as well as Anabell; both are All-America Rose Selections. One is Shreveport, named after the location of the national headquarters of the American Rose Society. Shreveport is a grandiflora with a growth habit much like Anabell's, but with a more nicely colored bloom—more subtle and grading toward yellow. Another worthy orange is Marina, which has vastly superior foliage to either of the others. All of these roses are thorny, have similar growth habits, and produce their best blooms in sprays.

Anabell is a prolific bloomer. While sprays that need disbudding occur most of the time, there will be a fair number of single blooms. Blossoms are small, but nicely formed, sweetly fragrant, and amazingly long lasting. Many prefer them fully open.

Foliage is dull but clean, and the bush is a real grower. You'll leave many more canes on this rose after pruning than most floribundas, and the vigor of the variety will support them. I've seen other rosarians' bushes of Anabell that are three times the size of mine. I prune mine low because I have a lot of wind to contend with and too much staking would be required if the bush got very tall. Also, a lot of the canes produce unmanageable sprays. Even after pruning, each season's growth will produce bushes taller than I can possibly let stand.

Angel Face
(Circus x Lavender Pinocchio) x Sterling Silver

When Gladys Fisher hybridized Sterling Silver for introduction in 1957, she became one of the most important women to the rose since

Empress Josephine by offering mauve as a color for modern roses. Since then, the mauve color class has progressed to the point that its modern parent, Sterling Silver, is no longer considered a strong contender for a mauve rose. The ARS now rates it at 4.8 (lower than 6.0 is called "of questionable value"). I'd rate it even lower for its pitiful performance, and I dug up all of mine some years ago. Although people still ask for it, I believe it is mainly because they remember its rather catchy name and sumptuous fragrance. They don't know that some of Sterling Silver's grandchildren have even finer fragrance and growth habits far superior to their predecessor. Foremost is Angel Face, hybridized by southern California's Swim and Weeks in 1968, and the All-America Rose Selection for 1969—the first mauve rose to earn this award.

Mauve is still not a color for everyone. I resisted it at first because of its funereal hue. I've since learned to respect it as a deserving color class, and if you get to that point, you can't resist Angel Face. First, as long as it's mauve, it's at least clear, not muddied. And the fragrance! It is virtually as strong as any modern rose.

Buds are lovely and high centered. They open into four-inch flat blooms with wavy petals around a center of golden stamens. Blooms keep well, even fully opened. Angel Face has irresistible displays of typical floribunda virtuosity with its multiple blooms on one stem, often in all stages of development.

Although others grow large bushes of Angel Face, mine are small. I believe the fact that I cut almost every bloom that appears *must* be a factor.

Besides being low-growing, the bushes have a spreading tendency. They're covered in coppery green foliage that's more disease-resistant than most.

Paradise

Swarthmore x Unnamed seedling

Here's a hybrid tea toward which hardly anyone is ambivalent. For some, it's a color too weird to have around. For others, it's too amazing to live without. Whichever, I wish *I* had hybridized it, but Ollie Weeks did, and earned an All-America Rose Selection in 1979. It's silvery lavender, splashed with ruby red on the petal edges and in random blotches into the bloom. Besides being one of the most unusual color combinations in modern rosedom, it's fragrant. Finally, it has incredible form. Even the smallest of blooms will have twenty-six to thirty petals perfectly arranged around a bull's-eye center.

What's wrong with it? The bush and the foliage. Leaves are a rather noncommittal green, prone to mildew. The threat of mildew doesn't worry me; I can control that. Preventive spraying, though, leads to another problem—the foliage begins to look as if you've taken a torch to it. In fact, all you did was spray with the same solution you used on your other bushes, and they look fine. The cause of this unfortunate reaction to spray still eludes me. But I'll continue to grow Paradise, and so will you if it takes your fancy.

There's a tendency for the bush to die back, as discussed in Chapter 4. You can cope with that fortunately since the bush is a strong grower and a heavy producer.

Paradise will fit quite nicely into the latest addition to the color classificaton of the ARS, mauve blend. If you had seen it in a rose show before this class was available, your natural tendency would have been to move it someplace else. Now it will seem at home with the likes of Patsy Cline, a recent Armstrong introduction. I predict that other roses will quickly join this color class—it's popular right now, and those who like it, get to be nuts about it.

Peace
{(George Dickson x Souvenir de Claudius Pernet)

x

(Joanna Hill x Charles P. Kilham)}

x

Margaret McGredy

If Peace were to come along today, I doubt that it would make a very big splash or become an All-America Selection. The fact is, however, that Peace's arrival could not have been more perfectly timed to make it the most famous rose in the world. Starting with its parentage, this rose has quite a history. It was the ultimate accomplishment of its hybridizer, Francis Meilland of France. Peace budwood was spirited from France on some of the last planes to leave before World War II occupation. It survived to become the floral symbol of the United Nations' formation in San Francisco in 1946 and was the All-America Selection the same year. Today it's still one of the top ten exhibition roses in the United States.

I think of Peace as a yellow, although it's classified by the ARS as a blend. In fact, no two blooms are alike, and this is part of Peace's enduring charm. I've seen the basic color so pale that it's really off-white, with edges dipped in pink. Sometimes, though, usually in the fall, its color is a deep clear yellow turning to coral orange at petal edges.

Here's a rose I definitely like better past the bud stage, preferably three-quarters open. The color variations add to its appeal for exhibition, and its form can be exemplary. It's considered slightly fragrant, though this is hardly why you'd buy it. Bushes are medium height and strong growers. Foliage is dark and shiny. It should be grown for one bloom per stem; sprays are disappointing by comparison. It will remain a favorite forever, if for sentimental reasons alone.

Gold Medal

Yellow Pages x Shirley Laugharn

Here's a rose whose success testifies to the fallibility of the present All-America Rose Selection process. It was passed over in 1983 when Sweet Surrender and Sun Flare won instead. Both of those selections, I predict, will be but vague memories in another decade. But not Gold Medal, and thank goodness the buying public recognized it for the winner it is. When Jack Christensen hybridized Gold Medal, he gave us a color we sorely needed. Not many yellows are great performers, but this one's a workhorse, producing scads of rich, yellow, fragrant blooms.

The bush itself is terrific. It's hardy, nicely shaped, and won't pout if you prune it rather low. If you prune it high, which it actually prefers, it will still reward you with bowers of bloom. For this versatility, it's a great landscape rose. Foliage is abundant, large, mid-green, and about as disease-resistant as that growing on any modern rosebush.

Buds are golden yellow with tawny edges. Blooms last on or off the bush, making it a favorite for those who want garden display or cut flowers.

Gold Medal is one of the best-behaved grandifloras around—it will do as it's told. If you like sprays, you can have them with long stems and multiple blooms. If you disbud properly, they're show-stoppers. If one to a stem is your thing, you can have them too, and they'll have exhibition form and impressive stem length. I like both and have some of each on all bushes.

Last Christmas I went out into the field with rather dim hopes of finding roses. It had already turned cold and had rained incessantly the preceding weeks. Most of the bushes had given up their last bloom more than a month earlier. Then I got to the Gold Medal bed. I cut two-to-three-foot stems (I could afford to; I was about to prune, and the bushes were over my head), most of them sprays. It's true I had to shake them upside down after I cut them since they were brimming with water. Once I put them in a large container, people looked at the Christmas tree only after they had rolled their eyes over Gold Medal.

So far Gold Medal is my pick for the rose of the eighties.

BEST BETS AT A GLANCE
Keep in mind that entries on this chart are the varieties that I suggest you grow. When you read that a bush is disease-prone with dull foliage and erratic blooms, you may wonder what it's doing here in the first place. But wait until you get a load of blossoms from one of these problematical varieties! Then you'll forgive the bush's shortcomings.

Remember, too, that height, disease-resistance, and bush and bloom characteristics are reported for where I grow roses—in a temperate climate. You may be blessed with more heat, meaning that rose varieties with more petalage will open their blossoms for you. Or your winters may be harsh and your growing season short, in which case your bushes won't have enough growing time to reach towering heights or to provide many successions of bloom.

VARIETY	COLOR	CLASSIFICATION	HEIGHT
MISTER LINCOLN	Dark red	Hybrid tea	3–4 feet
FRAGRANT CLOUD	Orange red	Hybrid tea	3–4 feet
PRECIOUS PLATINUM	Medium red	Hybrid tea	5–6 feet
EUROPEANA	Dark red	Floribunda	2–3 feet
DUET	Medium pink	Hybrid tea	3–4 feet
DAINTY BESS	Light pink	Single hybrid tea	3–4 feet
AQUARIUS	Pink blend	Grandiflora	4–5 feet
QUEEN ELIZABETH	Medium pink	Grandiflora	6–9 feet
CHERISH	Medium pink	Floribunda	2–3 feet
ROYAL HIGHNESS	Light pink	Hybrid tea	4–6 feet
SIMPLICITY	Medium pink	Floribunda	3–5 feet
PASCALI	White	Hybrid tea	3–4 feet
PRISTINE	White	Hybrid tea	4–6 feet
ICEBERG	White	Floribunda	4–5 feet
COLOR MAGIC	Pink blend	Hybrid tea	3–5 feet
DOUBLE DELIGHT	Red blend	Hybrid tea	3–4 feet
FIRST PRIZE	Pink blend	Hybrid tea	3–4 feet
GRANADA	Red blend	Hybrid tea	3–4 feet
SEA PEARL	Pink blend	Floribunda	4–6 feet
ANABELL	Orange-red	Floribunda	3–5 feet
PEACE	Yellow blend	Hybrid tea	3–4 feet
GOLD MEDAL	Deep yellow	Grandiflora	4–6 feet
ANGEL FACE	Mauve	Floribunda	2–3 feet
PARADISE	Mauve	Hybrid tea	3–4 feet

DISEASE-RESISTANCE	FOLIAGE	FRAGRANCE	BUSH CHARACTERISTICS	BLOOM CHARACTERISTICS
Average	Not notable	Lush	Urnlike	Semi-prolific
Poor	A bit oversize	Almost sinful	Dense	Dependable producer
Good	Abundant and shiny	Moderate	Large in girth	Scads of blossoms
Average	Mahogany to dark green	Disappointing for a red	Low and sprawling	Best in sprays
Good	Large, shiny, and unevenly spaced	Good	Awkward	Profuse, will spray
Average	Lighter green than most	Surprisingly strong	Spindly	Best in sprays
Good	Dark, matte green	Mediocre	Nicely shaped	Smaller-than-average blooms
Terrific	Large and dark	Light-moderate	Stately	Fabulous sprays
Strong	Abundant, thick, and toothed	Average	A ground-hugger	Perfect sprays
Prone to mildew	Dark and glossy	Delicate	Tall urns	Knockout buds
Average	Mid-green	Fair	Columnar, a natural for hedging	Abundant sprays, some one-to-a-stem blooms
Good	Olive to dark green and sparse	So-so	Nice shape	Best one to a stem, smallish
Good	Mahogany to dark green and large	Pleasant	Vicious thorns on a voracious grower	Profuse gardenia-shaped blossoms
Susceptible	Light to olive green	Moderate	Well shaped, good for landscaping	Prolific sprays
Average	Large and shiny	Crisp and clean	Dies back	Dinner-plate size blossoms
Poor	Unobtrusive	Heady	Thick, compact	Plenty
Vulnerable	Dark, matte green	Just detectable	Squat but substantial	Abundant, huge blooms
Weak	Serrated and decorative	Robust	Awkward	Steady
Good	Mid-green and well spaced	Moderate	Shapely	Long-lasting sprays
Good	Matte, mid-green	Sweet	Lots of fully clothed canes	Large, many-blossomed sprays
Moderate	Waxy and dark	Nonexistent	Rotund	No two blooms alike
Good	Matte, mid-green	Definite	Strong grower	Both one-to-a-stem blossoms and sprays
Susceptible	Proportionately small to bush	Heavy	Difficult to get height	Best in sprays
Poor	Not notable	Mild	Erratic	Lots of blossoms, all with form

CHAPTER 10
Other Notable Roses

Taking Exception to Ratings

You may recall that I suggested using the *Handbook for Selecting Roses* for a reference in buying roses. In that publication, a numerical rating system derived from members' votes assigns every rose a score from 1.0 to 10.0. Generally, look for roses with scores higher than 7.9, since 8.0 is the beginning of "Excellent." I agree with the ARS's ratings above 8.0 for the twenty-four roses I've just recommended, but I take great exception to other ratings—some are too low, others are too high.

The Underrated

Roses get poor ratings from voting members of the ARS primarily for their unsatisfactory performance in exhibition. It's true that the ones I'm listing in the next couple of pages may not do well enough at the show table to suit everybody. Still, I wouldn't think of being without them in my garden, and neither will you if you plant and rate them for yourselves.

Bewitched has been one of the prettiest pink roses around since it was introduced in 1967. One of the reasons for its low rating is its tendency to produce blooms with crooked necks. Remember, though, that a crooked neck is not a weak neck and that it can hold a bloom erect. Even in competition judges tend to overlook crooked necks when blossoms are worthy of award.

One of Bewitched's great assets is the purity of its color. It's fresh pink throughout, and the form of the bloom is lovely even when the blossoms are exceptionally large, as they're prone to be. Bewitched is intensely fragrant, and its foliage is glossy olive green and of average disease-resistance. The bush is nicely shaped.

You'll understand how sincere I am in believing that these roses are underrated when I tell you that Bewitched is my firm recommendation for someone who wants to grow a pink rose. Once I'm sure people want pink, not a blend, Bewitched is second to none.

I'm not certain why *White Lightnin'* doesn't have the rating it deserves. In 1980, when it became the first white grandiflora to win an All-America award, it seemed on the road to stardom. Again it's possible that hard-nosed judges are the culprits. You will recall that all the roses on a grandiflora spray should be at the same stage of bloom. White Lightnin' performs like a floribunda (which it should have been classified as in the first place) and shows stages of bloom all on one stem.

Whatever the causes for the disparaging rating, I couldn't agree with it less, and neither will you when you cut the blooms it gives freely. White Lightnin's mother is Angel Face. You can see the resemblance when you compare the blooms of the two varieties. White Lightnin' has wavy petals like those of its female parent. Also like Angel Face, it has great fragrance, in this case a unique, quite citruslike scent. The bush is of medium height (short for a grandiflora), but that doesn't hinder production. White Lightnin' is a bloomer, and both sprays and one-to-a-stem blooms appear simultaneously. Form is terrific either way.

Although *Brandy* was an All-America Selection in 1981, it has only a 7.3 rating today. It deserves higher. Brandy's bush is upright and perfectly shaped, with canes that head in the right direction to form an urn around a free interior center. The foliage is attractive and nicely shaped—about as much as you could want from a hybrid tea.

Brandy's bloom is elegant and aptly named. The golden apricot petals are shapely, and blooms appear with high centers and exhibition form. The fact that there are only twenty-five to thirty petals could account for its disappointing rating, especially if a lot of exhibitors cast their votes after warm weather has caused blooms to blow at the show table.

I think Brandy is a real winner whether or not it exhibits well. Besides, it has a fragrance that nicely fits its attractive color.

National Trust, I'm certain, is underrated because it doesn't grow well everywhere and because its blooms are often too small. If you grow it where the thermometer rarely tops 100 degrees, though, it's wonderful.

When I tell you that National Trust has no fragrance, you know that it must have something big going for it. It does—its form. National Trust has a way of quilling its petals as though the world's best rose groomer had taken a camel-hair brush to coax it to the limit. And for all its individuality, National Trust looks good with other roses; its highly distinct form doesn't clash with anything.

The bush is vigorous, and canes are plentiful but thorny. The foliage isn't particularly distinctive, but neither is it disease-prone.

National Trust buds are often unappealing. They tend to look malformed and too black at petal edges. As they open, the form works itself out to perfection and the color becomes a rich ruby red.

Although it's the highest rated of my underrated, not enough people know about *Just Joey*. The color, buff apricot, is a sure-fire winner. Better yet, blooms are powerfully fragrant and oversize.

Unfortunately, the bush can't seem to live up to the bloom. It's squat and never has the vigor you hope for. Its foliage is a nice dark green, but not particularly distinctive. Stems tend to be short and crooked.

I asked a very good florist who buys almost all the Just Joey we take to market why she liked it so much despite its persistently crooked stems. She exclaimed that's *why* she likes it so much—because it arranges itself in displays.

Just Joey lasts and lasts as a cut flower, and it never loses its fragrance. It's breathtaking fully open.

Medallion is underrated for the last reason you'd expect—it's oversize. When someone tells me they want to grow a huge, fragrant rose of a smart color, I suggest Medallion.

Apricots were popular as old roses, but they came a little late in the hybridizing of modern roses. Once they caught on and there were plenty for parenting, however, apricots and their blends gained rapidly in popularity. Almost all are fragrant.

Medallion is a nice bush too. It's vigorous, tall, shapely, and covered in medium green foliage. It has a spreading quality that's nice for keeping long-stemmed roses out of each other's way.

Medallion buds are very long. You have to wait for more than unfurled sepals to cut this bloom. The bud itself must begin unfurling and show its first row of petals clearly apart from the center before you cut, or Medallion won't open. Taken from the bush at the right time, it may very well get to be the biggest rose you've ever seen.

The Overrated

Roses get to be overrated because of sentiment and familiarity.

People are comfortable with roses they know the names of. For them every orange rose is Tropicana, all mauves are Sterling Silver, and reds are Chrysler Imperial.

It seems churlish to make disparaging remarks about a variety that performed wonderfully during all the years when we didn't have another rose with its particular color, fragrance, size, or blooming characteristics, but loyalty is out of place here. I believe that roses that have been conclusively outclassed by new introductions should have their ratings lowered.

I might as well begin with the most overrated of all, *Tropicana*. I can't imagine how Tropicana has bamboozled the public for so long. All those people who know its name are unaware that scads of orange roses have come along that outclass Tropicana by a mile.

I realize that detecting fragrance in a rose is often like finding beauty in a person's face—it depends on who's doing the looking, or in this case, the smelling. Some swear Tropicana is fragrant. I get nothing.

Other than being one of the first orange roses of exhibition quality, Tropicana has done nothing to deserve its popularity. I think its bloom is dumpy and the bush a mess. New canes appear only every third year for me, so I keep having bushes with wood that looks way past its time. It not only mildews and rusts, but it's the only variety that has ever blackspotted on me. To Tropicana, I say no, never.

Sunsprite is irresistibly yellow and smells wonderful, but its desirable qualities stop there. I'm picking on Sunsprite because it has a couple of habits I detest—it has no lasting qualities, and it drops its petals in a big hurry.

I can only guess that those responsible for its 8.9 rating are exhibitors with fifty bushes of Sunsprite. With that number they have a chance of catching blooms at the right time. Otherwise, the fleeting qualities of this rose will drive you mad. A whole spray can blow in a single day of warm weather.

I don't mind roses that drop their petals when they're really done, but Sunsprite is embarrassingly premature. A bloom you spot in the morning and think about cutting all day may have dropped its petals on the ground by the time you get home.

Chrysler Imperial has stayed around because of its very catchy, classy name. It deserved its selection as an All-America rose in 1953. After it became the dark red rose to beat, it began mothering and fathering some great offspring, most notably Mr. Lincoln. Over the years, many dark reds (National Trust, Precious Platinum, Toro) have come along that should have pushed Chrysler Imperial to the side of the road. It *is* fragrant, but that's about it. On the downside there's mildew on already-dull foliage, lack of vigor, and short stems. Finally, it blues at it ages more than any dark red I know.

I've been tempted to conclude that those responsible for its bafflingly high rating all live in hot climates, where Chrysler Imperial supposedly performs better (it has up to fifty petals), but that can't be it, because there are so many reds that do well for those growers. I still think it's the name.

Garden Party is another rose that should begin a slow fade toward retirement; it has been soundly replaced. Until 1978, if you asked any rosarian worth his salt to recommend a white rose with lavender-pink petal edges, he should have said Garden Party without deliberation. After Pristine came along, the answer was different.

Garden Party is still in there fighting to be a show rose, but it's losing. It has dropped from third to fourth place among exhibition roses in the last five years. Many people seem to grow Garden Party well. Actually, my *blooms* are good; it's the bush that's all wrong—it's the most rampant mildewer I know.

If you want this color, and I can't imagine why you wouldn't, trust me and try Pristine.

Miss All American Beauty was first known as Maria Callas. That name makes it difficult for me to deliver the remarks I'm about to. Madame Callas was my idea of a great diva. The name didn't work in this country as it had in Europe, so it was changed to Miss All American Beauty. Good name, bad rose.

If you want a huge, hot pink rose and you don't care how many "centers" it has, MAAB, as it's called, is for you. If you don't mind short stems, that helps too.

Maria Callas (I use *this* name when I have something nice to say) has great foliage; it's a nice dark green that looks impervious to disease, which it is, sort of. I have had blooms that made me gawk at their bold perfection, but for every one of those, I've had thirty blooms that looked like cabbages, each with so many centers that they gave me headaches.

I call *Folklore* "Rosa vulgaris." Now, I'm into size, but I want large *blooms*, not gargantuan bushes. I can't tell you how many pictures I've seen of rosarians' wives perched on top of stepladders cutting blooms of Folklore. It's unquestionably the tallest hybrid tea around (it does make a great living, impenetrable hedge). If you're fond of skyscraping bushes, plant Folklore. Otherwise, you should know about the problems. Remember balance and proportion in exhibiting? Folklore scores a zero. Blooms mature on very long stems. Even if you cut with the bush in mind, blooms are disproportionately small compared to their stems.

The pluses are mainly a pleasant fragrance and a color that is a distinctive blend of yellow and shrimp pink. The bush is disease-resistant, but who cares?

Follies

When people ask me which roses I grow, I rattle off varieties that I'm sure will meet with their approval—Queen Elizabeth, Mister Lincoln, Pristine, Iceberg—as many of my best bets as my memory can dredge up. I never volunteer the names of those varieties that I know would raise some eyebrows among fellow rosarians.

All serious rose aficionados I've ever met grow at *least* one rose variety that they know they really shouldn't. A friend of mine pampers his Tropicana even though he knows perfectly well that more-recent orange roses put it to shame. Some people grow inferior varieties because they're loyal to the first roses they ever planted themselves. Other gardeners stubbornly persevere with puny bushes simply because their occasional blooms are *exactly* what they think a rose should look like. My pet folly is Alabama.

Here's what *Modern Roses 9* has to say about Alabama:

> HT. (Weeks; int. Weeks Wholesale Rose Grower, '76.) Mexicana × Tiffany. Bud long pointed, globular; fl. large (3½–4 in.) dbl. (25 petals), high centered to cupped, fragrant (tea), pink, white. Fol. dark, leathery. Upright; intermittent bloom. Pl. Pat. 4008. pink blend.

Here's what I have to say about Alabama: when it's on, which is far too seldom, it's stupendous. It makes me take another look at Color Magic, my admitted favorite rose. Like Color Magic, Alabama is a pink blend, only darker. It's also the quintessential English Box rose. Large blossoms that look as though they're made of taffeta swirl their intense rose pink petals around a bull's-eye center.

In stating that Alabama's bloom is intermittent, *Modern Roses 9* is being particularly kind. Stingy is more like it. Its bushes go into remission and act as if they don't know that they're supposed to re-bloom. When they finally do, their blossoms usually have crooked or weak necks. But every so often, they remember how to get everything together, and, oh my, what a bloom!

The other evening I came in from the cutting field cradling a basket of roses in my left arm and holding an Alabama queen in my right hand. "Here," I announced, "is why we grow Alabama," as I held the stately stem for all the processors to see. "Where's the rest?" a particularly snippy processor asked. "Oh, they had weak necks or just weren't right," I answered. "And *that's* why we shouldn't grow it," he retorted. I knew he had me; there was no use arguing.

I know countless people who grow Cecile Brunner, some who say it's their favorite rose and that is was their grandmother's too. For my taste, Cecile Brunner is insipid, but I've learned not to say that to those who cultivate this son of a polyantha.

If you've fallen in love with some obscure rose for whatever reason seems okay to you, have it. Just don't get carried away. I'd be in sad shape if I had to depend on Alabama for a steady supply of flowers. So I keep just a few bushes and secrete them among reliable bloomers.

Miniatures

I want to be very careful with this subject because I don't wish to offend good friends who grow miniature roses. "Minis," as they're called, just aren't for me, and not because I think it's unbecoming for a grown man to talk about his Cuddles, Puppy Love, Toy Clown, or Baby Betsy McCall. I know a good number of fine rosarians who have only token bushes of my kinds of roses—all their gardening space is devoted to miniatures. To them I say fine, and I promise to try not to be disparaging as long as they respect my preference.

Miniature roses aren't known for their fragrance. In fact, only a few are considered to have any distinct scent at all. I have some minis in my garden because I like to give large sprays of blooms to friends who love them. A more practical reason is that we've found that dried whole they're great for potpourri (the addition of essential oils will perfume even scentless dried materials). The few I do grow are budded as tree roses; otherwise, I would have to practically sit on the ground to maintain them.

There are some good reasons for growing miniatures, however. Space is one. Minis can be grown successfully in containers. I know a woman who has more than one hundred lining the exterior fire escape on her apartment building. Other people without garden space grow miniatures in pots on window ledges, on back stoops, and in sunny spots they find around the house. Miniatures also tend to be hardier and more disease-resistant than their larger relatives. Many people choose them because they don't want to use any chemical sprays (although miniature bushes are prone to heavy spider-mite infestation).

If you decide to grow miniatures, you have an incredible number of varieties from which to select. The market is glutted with them, for once they caught on, they spread like gossip. The six I'm recommending hardly scratch the surface of those available (the 1985 *Handbook for Selecting Roses* lists thirty-eight other highly rated miniatures). I've selected these varieties because they're good performers, they represent a wide color selection, and they're among the miniatures I grow.

After Peace, *Starina* may go down in history as the most famous rose from the Meillands of France. It has a 9.6 rating by the ARS! The color is orange-red, and blooms appear freely, usually in sprays. Foliage is abundant and disease-resistant. Starina is tough to beat in competition and has been in first place among the minis for more than ten years.

If I could grow only one miniature, *Popcorn* would be my choice, perhaps because its bloom is single. I can appreciate this form better than that of minis with more petals that I can't see well enough to fairly evaluate. Blooms are white, and petals surround a center of golden stamens. When the bushes come a cropper (bloom all at once), which they often do, it looks as though someone has tossed a batch of freshly popped corn onto a tough little green bush.

Magic Carrousel is white with red edgings. Its foliage is small, glossy, and leathery. This mini has a lovely mother—Little Darling, one of the highly rated floribundas. Besides being prolific, Magic Carrousel's blossoms last exceptionally well. Fortunately for us, blooms dry nicely and retain their blended colors, making them dramatic accents in potpourri.

Holy Toledo is a nice name for a nice miniature. The bloom is a brilliant apricot-orange with a yellow-orange reverse on the petals. We grow this mini as a tree rose. When bushes are in full bloom, covered in large sprays, they make an arrangement all on their own. Blooms last and dry beautifully.

Lavender Jewel was squired by Angel Face and is a clear lavender-mauve. *Modern Roses* 9, the bible for the registration statistics of roses, lists it as slightly fragrant; but try as I might, I can smell nothing (I think everyone believes it *should* be scented because of its famous fragrant father). Bushes grow to be quite large and are forever in bloom.

Yellow Doll also is aptly named. Depending on how much sun there is, the basic bright yellow color can shade to cream. This mini has fifty to sixty petals, which is more than most, but they're narrow. It is also listed as fragrant, but I wouldn't buy it for that quality. Nor would I plant Yellow Doll if I wanted to exhibit, for once blooms begin opening, they lose form rapidly.

Even though they've still not won my heart, when I analyzed last season's weekly computer readouts of how our blooms fared at the flower market, I realized that I could no longer grow only a handful of miniature roses—they always sell. I gave in to planting more. I decided to try some of the newer varieties that haven't yet stood the test of time, some so recent they have not been rated by voting members of the ARS.

Begrudgingly, I telephoned a supplier who knows that I think minis are terminally cute. I told him that as long as I was going to grow more miniatures, I wanted hardy varieties that bloomed freely in the best-selling color range: white and pastels. "Do you care how tall they get?" he asked. I assured him the taller the better. "Then you'll like *Jean Kenneally*," he informed me, "because it will rise above everything else." My minimentor was right; Jean Kenneally is definitely my pick of the litter. Named for a fine southern California rosarian, Jean Kenneally is a skyscraper among miniatures (my plants reached three feet their first year in the ground). Bushes produce large sprays of light apricot blooms on long stems. Hardcore mini fanciers, especially those who prefer microminis, may turn up their noses, but I like her just fine.

Also at my supplier's suggestion, I planted *Minnie Pearl*, a variety that grows nearly as tall as Jean Kenneally and has blooms almost the same color, only pinker. He suggested *Pacesetter* as our white, another good choice. Finally, because practically everyone likes the color, I also planted *Little Sir Echo*, a clear, midpink. Its blooms are okay, but the bushes are puny compared to those of the more vigorous varieties.

Standards

Modern rosebushes, as you know, are two separate varieties grafted together at the bud union. The rootstock is the portion underground, and the hybrid is the portion growing above the bud union. In standards, a third variety is introduced between the two—just a cane of rosewood along whose length nothing is intended to grow; it simply provides height for the hybrid growing on top.

Standards are often called tree roses; they can be anywhere from eighteen inches to three feet tall—even taller if custom budded. Standards are fine for landscaping and as a means of squeezing in additional roses when your garden has room for roots below; but not for bushes above. Since the major growth will be above them, tree roses can be planted right between two large bushes.

When I first grew roses, I was told that tree roses produce blooms with better form than bushes of the same variety, so I planted lots of them. They don't, in fact, yield superior blooms, and their cutting stems are likely to be shorter than those of bushes.

I know a rosarian who buds his own rose trees and grafts two hybrids of different colors on top of the support trunk. He has a dozen trees, each budded with both National Trust and Pascali, planted in a chamomile lawn with a croquet court snaking in and around them (very Alice in Wonderland). He has some secret that he has not yet divulged (I think he plans to will it to me) for getting both varieties to bloom at the same time. It is quite a sight.

I don't like standards of varieties known to grow large; they get top-heavy. I think staking looks crude, but if you don't do something, you open yourself up to heartache when the wind breaks off whole canes. For this reason, many floribundas make good standards, as do the more average size hybrid teas, and they can be kept nicely shaped.

Catalogues list the rose varieties available as standards, and many offer a wide selection. If you fall in love with a rose that isn't available as a tree, many nurseries, particularly those specializing in roses, will bud it for you.

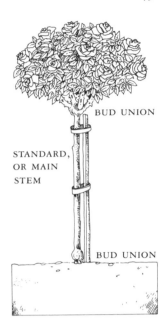

BUD UNION

STANDARD, OR MAIN STEM

BUD UNION

STANDARDS
Standards , *or tree roses, have two bud unions separated by a stretch of rose wood with nothing growing along it. At the top a hybrid is grafted; at the base is rootstock. Standards are good solutions for squeezing in more rosebushes when your garden has room for roots below, but not for bushes above.*

CLIMBERS
Some climbers were hybridized to sprawl; others are just climbing versions of conventional bushes. No matter which type, ramblers must be trained to grow where you want them; their growth is aimless, and they have no tendrils for attaching themselves. Whatever pattern you create, be sure to tie down the tips, thereby encouraging blooms all along climbers' arching canes.

Climbers

Climbing roses are wonderful if you have the right places to train them. Roses don't climb in the usual sense because they have no tendrils for attaching themselves to what they're growing on. Modern climbers must be trained over what they grow on to shape them properly. Solid walls aren't good because they prevent air circulation. Fences, even wire ones, are perfect, since all you really need is some place to attach them for height and lateral growth.

If you consider planting climbers, commit this to memory: They must always be trained to arch their canes with tips pointing downward. This shaping technique causes sap to travel the full length of canes and encourages blooms on stems all the way along. Besides, trained this way, they're very pretty on a trellis wall or fence even when not in bloom. When they do flower, usually as a cropper, they're a blaze of color.

When I planted my first climber, I trained it on a garden railing. The railing is ideal in that it has posts every three feet and four equally spaced horizontal boards running the entire length. I used fencing staples to attach the canes. Wrong. While the canes fit comfortably within the constraints of the holder when I attached them, two years later they had grown thicker than the metal constraints and were damaged. Now I use the same heavy staple, but I tie a short length of expandable garden tape to it and the other end to a climbing cane. This arrangement allows canes to expand their girth comfortably.

Before I recommend three specific climbers, let me give you a broader hint. Sometimes rose varieties that have always grown on a bush will up and start growing like a climber. Budwood is taken from these new growth variations, and if it tests out in trial growing conditions, it will be introduced as a climbing version of its parent. Some great varieties have developed climbing versions of themselves. Of the roses in my best-bet section, there are climbing renditions of Dainty Bess, Queen Elizabeth, Double Delight, First Prize, and Angel Face. Sometimes a climbing version will outperform the bush from which it developed. I have bushes of a rose called Sutter's Gold that perform so-so, but the climber is stupendous. Rosarians get bad reputations for exaggeration, like fishermen or some Texans, but I swear it had 144 blooms on it at one time.

Otherwise, you might consider:

America, the rose world's gift to the Bicentennial, is the only climbing rose ever chosen All-America. Probably because Fragrant Cloud is its mother, America is sharply fragrant. America is classified as an orange-red because there isn't a class for coral, the true color. It has forty to fifty petals, which distinguish themselves by their perfectly symmetrical arrangement, even in fully open blooms.

I like apricot as a color for roses. *Royal Sunset* is a climber of such hue that is an august grower and producer. Sutter's Gold is the father, so it has abundant fragrance. The foliage is dark leathery green, and the quick-repeat blooming cycle is a real plus.

No one can seem to decide what to call *Altissimo*, nor how to train it. Should it be treated as a climber, a pillar, or a large flowering shrub? No matter. It's a terrific blood red, seven-petaled single with golden stamens, and a house eater when trained on a trellis or as a pillar. To top it off, it's very fragrant and lasts on or off the plant for an amazing length of time.

CHAPTER 11
Special Culturing

Roses in Containers

If you have no garden for planting rosebushes in the earth, but do have patio, deck, or even exterior stairway space available, you can still have roses. In fact, roses in containers require care only incidentally different from those planted in the ground. The rewards can be great, even greater, as when you are asked, "How did you ever do it in just a planter?"

Which roses will grow in containers? Virtually all of them, but rosebushes that tend to be on the small side of average will do best. Miniatures are a snap, of course, but your rose world certainly needn't be restricted to minis. Floribundas do beautifully, but so will the more diminutive hybrid teas, even grandifloras. Select carefully, choosing from those varieties that don't get to be huge. If you want clusters of pink blooms, think about Cherish rather than Queen Elizabeth, which will be top-heavy after the first year's growth. If you yearn for red one-to-a-stem blooms, opt for Mister Lincoln instead of Precious Platinum. If you just can't bear not having some vigorous grower that has won your heart, go ahead and plant it. Your love for the variety will probably motivate you to give it the extra care it will need to perform well in its restricted environment.

Love didn't motivate me to try one container experiment, but I think you should know about it anyway. You may recall that I had rather disparaging remarks to make about Folklore, one of the roses I contend is overrated. For some reason I once had a spare bush of it and an extra container as well. At the same moment I realized that the planter was too small for a rosebush, I thought: Why not try a Folklore experiment? Since Folklore planted in the garden gets to be unwieldy in size, it seemed that purposefully constricting its root development in an undersize container might keep it within bounds. It worked. At summer's end, my contained Folklore looked like a normal hybrid tea. Unfortunately, I can't report on second-year developments, for I found another use for the container more to my liking.

If you make your own containers, be sure to use one of the decay-resistant woods (cedar, cypress, or redwood). Don't skimp on size. Most container experts stipulate a minimum fourteen-inch width and depth. A few extra inches will prove worth the expense, especially after a year or more of growth, when extra root space is needed for the continuing development of the bushes.

Before you put the first trowelful of soil into a container, consider what the total weight is likely to be when you've finished planting. Containers large enough to accommodate roses are very heavy when filled with soil, even heavier when wet. Think carefully about where you're going to place it, choosing a spot you're certain will please you for a long time. If you're one of those people who likes frequent rearranging, you might consider attaching casters to the container bottom before planting. Then you can even move it around during the day, especially if you must do so to keep the bush in the sunlight. Don't laugh. I know someone who does just that. A formidable exhibitor in San Francisco has a weird backyard sun pattern, created by strangely shaped buildings to the east and west. She never gets sunlight for more than three hours on either side of her garden. All her roses (she admits to about fifty) are in containers with commercial casters equipped with stop-and-go locking foot pedals. You guessed it; she moves her rosebushes twice daily. You certainly can't quibble with her results. Neither can judges.

Once you are ready to plant, use decent soil. If you don't have a yard to plant in, it's unlikely you'll have soil available. Buy some. Use one of the packaged varieties—they really are a loose, friable growing medium.

It's hard to build a cone of soil within a planter, but the goal when planting in a planter is the same as that stated in Chapter 3 for planting in the earth—to position a rosebush and its roots where they will grow comfortably.

Put shards from clay pots or place rocks over the planter's drainage holes, then fill the bottom of the container with soil to a point where the bush can be added. You want the bud union to end up one inch above the soil level within the container and two inches from its lip.

I always thought that one of the benefits of container roses was that they could be wintered over indoors when outside temperatures dipped to dangerous lows. That apparently is not always the case. Capable rosarians who live in cruel winter climates tell me that basement and garage storage doesn't work particularly well and that container roses should be dug up yearly and planted outdoors in three-foot-deep trenches until spring signals their rejuvenation. Sounds torturous to me; not so much for the bushes as for the poor rosarians. But I know that if I suddenly had to deal with a regularly dipping thermometer, I too would develop a fetish for trenches. If you live where it's brutally cold and have no place for trenches, I suppose you'll just have to take containers in and out of doors until hard freezes are over.

Otherwise, care for container roses is the same as that given bushes planted in the garden. Container roses will need watering more often than their grounded siblings because containers drain rapidly and moisture evaporates from all sides. Feeding and pruning needs are identical to those for garden-grown bushes.

There *is* one additional periodic need. Bushes grown in containers for several years become "root bound," with root systems larger than their planters can allow. When that happens, growth becomes stunted. To remedy the situation, remove the bush while it's dormant and trim its roots back by half. Old, tough roots should come out entirely. Use the same techniques for replanting the bush that you used to plant it originally.

There's one more approach to growing roses in containers that I like. So might you if there's an out-of-the-way spot where no one has to see something out of bloom. I plant bushes in five-gallon sturdy plastic containers, which retain moisture well and don't allow roots to grow into their sides. Roots don't adhere to plastic as they do to wood, and bushes in plastic containers last longer than those in wooden ones. When a plant comes into bloom and is worth looking at, I move its container into a cachepot—a pretty temporary holding pot. When the show is over, I take the container out, return it to its sequestered growing area, and look around for something in bloom to take its place in the cachepot.

Landscaping with Roses

I prefer to keep roses in a section of the garden all their own rather than scattering them around. If you grow roses in a wide array of colors to enjoy their blooms indoors, think about giving the bushes their own space, maybe just a cutting section within your garden, where their hues and shades won't compete with whatever is nearby. However, if you have an empty trellis, arbor, fence, pergola, or if you want a hedge or border plantings, that's another matter, and you should sprinkle roses liberally throughout your landscape.

Besides those already mentioned, many climbing and pillar roses are fine for landscaping as long as you remember their colors when you plant them. When ramblers are in full bloom (and they usually blossom in flushes all at once), they make bold garden statements. Make sure that their vivid colors complement your other plantings.

When you plant a hedge or a border of ground-huggers, you have the best of two worlds since you can cut for the house *and* leave color on the bushes. I strongly urge you to plant only one variety, or at least only one color, in a row. Mixed colors look like a mishmash.

Sometimes one large rosebush makes an attractive landscape accent. Or you may want to hide something such as a utility meter or a water spigot. Besides giving thought to complementary colors, decide how tall or wide the bushes will have to get (remember also that roses go dormant and will expose your eyesore for a while). Varieties such as Queen Elizabeth grow to be exceptionally tall, and some more modern shrub varieties can grow into bushes the size of a small car, particularly the "parkroses" from Kordes of West Germany.

The prettiest rosebushes I've seen in a landscape form a color-coordinated row of standards planted along a winding walkway to the front porch of a stately home. Their proprietor, a man who swears he always knew that the rose would eventually become America's national flower, chose his favorite red, pink, and white All-America Rose Selections and had them budded as tree roses. A thick, spongy lawn grows to within a one-foot circle of the base of each plant and everything is as neat as a pin.

However much those of us who prefer modern roses hate admitting it, old garden roses are better for landscaping, especially if you have something too large for even the most rambunctious of modern hybrids to camouflage. If the outside of a shed is irrevocably ugly, but it harbors a useful interior, plant a house-eating old rose to gobble it up. Or if you buy an old home with an abandoned outhouse that you don't feel like moving, cover it with *Gold of Ophir*, the favorite rose of M. F. K. Fisher's childhood. Keep in mind that most older varieties have only one bloom. True, it's long and profuse, but that's it. Even so, foliage remains throughout most of the year, dropping only at pruning time, when even old roses go dormant.

Companion Planting

I have a book called *Roses Love Garlic*, which is all about plants liking certain other plants as neighbors. It offers several worthwhile suggestions, some of which I've followed in our fragrant garden, but not among my roses. It's true that roses like garlic growing next to them; garlic and its family repel aphids, and roses detest anything that sucks at their juices. I love garlic too, but you'll never catch me planting it or any edible herb or vegetable near my roses. I spray my bushes faithfully, and although I don't aim my poisons at anything else, misty fallout covers whatever is nearby anyway. If you don't spray at all, of course, you can plant anything consumable next to or under your roses.

The fact that rosebushes like to grow with a comfy blanket of mulch over their roots discourages most would-be neighbors. Roses are greedy. They want more than an even share of water and nutrients and resent the competition of other plants.

If you can't stand the sight of barren mulch, at least plant something shallow-rooted such as alyssum, dianthus, or pansies. Lobelia has short roots too, but if you plant one of the blue shades, think about how it will look underneath the rose colors you select. If you're in doubt, plant the white variety.

Keep whatever you plant out of the space between the center of the bush and its drip line. You'll bless this accessible territory when you water, apply fertilizers, or have to cut its blooms.

Two New Ways of Growing

Very soon we're going to be growing roses differently from the way we do now. There are two new ways you should know about. One approach has been around for a while, and it is simply being perfected. The other is in its infancy.

Roses on Their Own Roots

Rose varieties that grow on roots they develop themselves have long been touted to be superior to those grown conventionally on rootstock. When I first heard about them, I thought it was possible only with miniatures (minis grow on their own roots unless budded as standards). Then I learned that people took fresh wood from a bush they wanted to try growing on its own roots and planted it in containers or directly in the ground. Only recently have I learned that some varieties seem to grow better this way than they do when conventionally budded to rootstock.

You should know about a legal problem. Roses that are hybridized and introduced for commerce have a seventeen-year patent, during which time they cannot be asexually reproduced. Growing them on their own roots must be for personal use only.

Not having rootstock is a problem when cuttings first start out, since they can't develop massive root systems in a hurry. I bought some bushes growing on their own roots a few years ago. Their first year in the ground was thoroughly uneventful. During the second year, I began seeing possibilities. After three years, they're performing like their budded siblings. Time is the factor.

Getting cuttings to root properly requires some technique. Theoretically, rooting is possible any time of the year, but I wouldn't do it in the heat of summer without providing some shade. Since I like to root cuttings in the ground where they are to grow, I do it at pruning time when excess heat is no longer a worry. Commercial rooting stimulants are a big help. You simply immerse one end of a freshly cut stem into it before sticking the stem into the ground.

Five budding eyes per stem seem to be the magic number for successful rooting. Three eyes go underground. Either or both eyes left above soil level will sprout if the rooting takes. The soil in which cuttings are expected to root should be highly friable.

During the last pruning season I decided to try some varieties I've heard do well on their own roots. A college student who works for us part-time saw me doing it and suggested something I was embarrassed not to have thought of myself, since I had seen my grandmother do it many times. The idea was to place fruit jars over the cuttings. These glass shelters are a great boost for successful rootings. First, they protect tender new growth from crippling cold snaps. Second, they create a microclimate in which warm moisture seems to coax sprouting.

I've seen plants of Altissimo (which was introduced in 1966 and has lost its patent protection) that are bigger and healthier than any I've seen budded on rootstock. Try taking cuttings of any variety you like, but if the variety is younger than seventeen, don't try to peddle them.

Tissue Cultures in Vitro

Tissue culture is a process in which selected portions of a plant are grown on an artificial medium under sterile conditions. Cultures are grown in glass vessels, hence the name *in vitro*. Quick propagation of orchid species spurred early tissue-culture efforts. Other flowering plants have since been tried, and it was inevitable that successful cloning would extend to roses.

The first step for tissue culturing roses is the selection of bud eyes from virus-free bushes. Next is disinfestation, which rids cuttings of fungi and bacterial contamination. Once sterilized, buds are set upon an artificial medium within a sterile test tube.

The type of growth that develops from cultures is a function of the medium in which the buds are propagated. One formulation of nutrients, vitamins, and growth regulators encourages shoot development; another promotes roots.

Shoots are encouraged first. Several plantlets sprout from each bud eye within three weeks when light cycles, temperature, and humidity are all carefully controlled. Once sufficient shoots have developed, they are transferred to a new artificial medium formulated to encourage strong, healthy roots. When well rooted, the tiny rose plants are removed from their test tubes and planted in a greenhouse to acclimatize them to growing in a soil medium. After two to three months of greenhouse care, plants are ready for commerce in disposable plastic containers.

In America, tissue culturing of roses is being pioneered by Armstrong Nurseries. Its parent company, Moet-Hennesy, has constructed a laboratory in Somis, California, modeled after a similar facility operated by Delbard Nurseries of France.

I visited Armstrong Nurseries to see the experimental laboratories there and left with some established tissue cultures to evaluate in our growing field. I'm impressed with what they've done.

I planted the tissue cultures next to my rosebushes of the same varieties that are growing on conventional, budded rootstock. The first bush bloomed one day short of three weeks after planting! Such quick reward will surely be a good marketing feature, as will the fact that bushes are growing on their own roots, thereby never producing sucker growth. Finally, bushes that can be planted anytime during the growing season are certain to be more salable than those restricted to the comparatively short bareroot season.

Will tissue-cultured rosebushes replace the budded-onto-rootstock varieties? It's too soon to tell. Among other things, the impact on hybridizers' patenting protection must be resolved. We must also look at costs down the road. On the one hand, budding roses onto rootstock is painstakingly slow and labor intensive, making costs ever on the rise. Tissue culture, on the other hand, offers a method for more rapid plant reproduction at which is likely to be a fraction of current costs. The day may well come when we never buy another rosebush with a bud union on it.

Your Own Rose

There are two ways to get a rose all your own. First, nature might just up and reward you with a "sport." Second, you can create a great rose with hybridizing techniques that are easy to master.

Sports

Genetic throwbacks that occur spontaneously are called sports. Your bushes may sport just because you've maintained them so well.

Imagine a bush that delights you with bowers of white blossoms. Then one day when you go to cut, there in the midst of all that white bounty is a wonderful dark red rose. You did nothing deliberate to encourage this spontaneous event; nature did it all. Wonderful roses have begun just this way.

Woody growth that terminates in a bloom different from what is on the rest of the bush can develop anywhere on the plant. A new cane can stem from the bud union, a lateral can develop, or a stem may grow, any of which may harbor a mutant. The tricky part is deciding where the mutation has occurred so you don't cut it off. If a sport shows promise, you want to produce "budwood": fresh woody growth that can be budded onto rootstock.

The best thing to do to be sure the mutant isn't within what you cut off is to remove the finished bloom with no stem. You won't get strong new growth from your cut, but that's better than aborting the mutation. Wait for a new blossom, since the sport has to prove itself by duplicating its first bloom.

If the second bloom is as promising as the first, the sport should be budded. Contact a local nurseryman or consulting rosarian who will graft its wood onto rootstock for you, at least the first time.

We've had two sports worthy of consideration at Garden Valley Ranch, both on terrific parents. The first came on Duet and is a pale pink rose with Duet's foliage and growing habits. We've budded it onto rootstock and are evaluating it as a bush.

The second sport has considerably more potential. It came on Brandy, a wonderful apricot rose that won the All-America Rose Selection in 1980. The sport is a pure butter yellow, fragrant bloom that we haven't yet been able to test long enough. It came so late in the growing season that we had to let wood "live over" to the next year without pruning. It has since proven itself by blooming true to color a second time, and we've budded its wood for serious evaluation.

Hybridizing

Creating your own rose by mating male and female roses you choose to marry is easier than you might imagine. Anyone with two different rosebushes can do it.

Roses are bisexual. The selection of who squires and who receives is arbitrary; the female is the rose that remains on the bush, and the male is the one tossed after use. Blooms just beginning to open are at the right stage for hybridizing.

Prepare the female first, in case you break it off the bush, in which case it can serve as the male. Remove all petals, using the technique of snapping them off at their bases as described in the instructions for exhibiting (Chapter 7).

When you have depetaled the bloom, both sets of reproductive organs will be obvious. Female organs are centermost and consist of delicate stalks called pistils. Tips of pistils, stigmas, provide the spots for pollen deposits.

The male organs are taller and surround the pistils entirely. Slender male stalks are stamens, tipped by anthers, which hold pollen in capsule sacs.

All male parts must be removed from the female to avoid self-pollination. Anthers can be plucked off with tweezers or carefully cut off with a sharp knife. Try not to injure pistils while removing anthers.

After male parts have been removed, tie a paper bag over the female so no wanderlust pollen adheres to the sticky substance that will soon appear on stigmas.

The father can be cut from the bush to make further emasculation easier. Remove all petals and scrape anthers from stamens into the small vial (baby-food jars are perfect). If you must use gloves, use smooth-surfaced ones so all pollen will fall into the jar. Close the jars to prevent foreign invasion.

In one day, two at most, you're ready for the wedding ceremony. Unveil the bride by removing the bag; female stigmas will be sticky. In the jar, anthers will have ruptured from their sacs. Use an artist's camel-hair brush to collect the pollen inside the jars and apply it to the stigmas. If some of the capsules of pollen haven't burst yet, rub them on anyway; the sticky substance will break down the sac quickly. Put the bag back on.

For the cross to be fertile, sperm from the pollen must travel down the pistils to an ovule at their base that contains unfertilized eggs. Quite a little hideout for a honeymoon.

Be sure to label your cross right then; don't trust your memory. List the female parent first (it's traditional), and identify the cross as the pros would: _____ × _____. Put the date on as well.

The bag can come off after a couple of days. By then the stigmas will have lost their stickiness and will no longer be receptive to pollen. Now all you can do is cross your fingers, pray, project good Karma, or whatever works.

If the cross takes, the hip will stay green and start to swell in a few weeks. If your efforts prove barren, the hip will dry and fall off. Remember that percentages of "takes" are low even for the best of hybridizers, so don't be discouraged if your first crosses don't take.

The hip will ripen in three to four months and turn red, yellow, orange, or brown. Hips should be harvested as soon as they start to lose the freshness of whichever color they've turned.

Hips are carefully sliced open to reveal their seed(s); there may be only one or more than fifty. Store seeds in plastic baggies filled with damp peat moss and keep them refrigerated at under forty degrees for six weeks.

From here on I can't be of much help. I have only just started this process myself, and I'm experimenting with various stratified mediums and methods for germination. What I've learned has come from the Rose Hybridizers Association. You, too, will need their advice. Write to Larry D. Peterson, 3245 Wheaton Road, Horseheads, New York 14845. Something else you should do is read *The Makers of Heavenly Roses* by Jack Harkness; he tells engaging stories about seventeen of the world's most prestigious hybridizing clans.

Seeds properly stratified and planted will germinate and bloom in a couple of months. The first bloom won't be the last word on your new rose, but you can tell a lot from it. Color will be true, as will petal shape. If you're encouraged enough to go to the next step and bud the seedling onto rootstock, you may get increased petalage and fragrance.

It's useless to tell you, a new hybridizer, to be critical of your first seedlings. You'll tend to love them regardless of obvious flaws. And why not? They're yours. One thing is certain; the likelihood of your creating a new rose is as great as it is for those who have been trying hard for decades. That is because chance is an overwhelming factor. It's true that if you want to create a new red rose, you might as well select red mothers and fathers; the pros say you improve your odds by sticking with the colors you're after. But your crimson rose parents may also produce the purest white rose ever seen, or something in between.

If you do come up with a winner, contact the ARS and learn about the test program they sponsor for evaluating roses created by amateurs. You may become the proud parent of an All-America Rose.

Final Words

Too many roses are being put on the market. Some hybridizers introduce every new rose they develop, regardless of its promise. I made a pledge when I began hybridizing: I will never introduce a rose unless it has a unique color or more vigor, fragrance, or prolific blooming habits than those already in commerce. Why burden the market with your rose if it's indistinguishable from or not as good as those already available?

I'd like any rose I introduce to have fragrant large blooms in abundance. I really don't care what color it is, though I'd prefer something other than orange or mauve.

Alain Meilland of the famous French hybridizing family has declared that he is out to create the world's first blue rose. I don't think I'd like a blue rose. The color seems all wrong (maybe that's because I've not yet seen one). But whether I like blue roses or not, I'd love to hybridize one. Just about every breeder would like to, whether he or she admits it or not. I've got some secret ideas of how it might be done. So, Monsieur Meilland, the race is on.

The most beautiful rose I've ever seen came from my garden in San Francisco. It was a bloom of Chicago Peace, a fine rose that is nonetheless overrated by the ARS. It's too stingy with its blooms to suit me. Chicago Peace is a sport of Peace that has done a color reversal on its mother. It also is yellow and pink, but there's more pink; the yellow forms the edgings. The color combination alone might win your heart. If not, the ruffled petals surely will.

This particular bloom came from a new cane that I had snapped some six to eight weeks earlier. Even cutting for the bush, I came away with something longer than a two-foot stem heavily clothed in foliage. This was an exhibition bloom that would have set new standards for most judges coming across it in a show, particularly for its considerable size and balanced proportions. I was going to a dinner party that evening and knew that the hostess liked flowers, so I plunked it in a milk carton and took it along.

My friend truly appreciated the gesture, but she's one of those people to whom roses are roses. She likes them, mind you, but doesn't need star quality. She put it in a lovely crystal bud vase, but couldn't decide where to place it. Her mind was on the stroganoff simmering on the stove. Finally, she set it on a low side table with a tall lamp over it and went on with the dinner party as if nothing extraordinary had occurred. I happened to be seated kitty-corner from this miraculous flower. As I stole quick glances at it between snatches of conversation with the other guests, I noticed that the lighting not only showed the bloom to perfection, but that it was giving off just enough heat to coax my prize into classic exhibition form. I couldn't keep my eyes off it. When I left, I seriously debated whether to ask the hostess if I could take it with me and send her two dozen regular roses the next day. I restrained myself, barely.

If someone doesn't appreciate the fruits of your labors, don't be disappointed. You can't project your standards on others. We all do what we can to teach our friends to recognize magnificent roses when they see them, but educating the public takes a lot of time. Until those around you give you the praise you deserve, you might consider exhibiting; judges will recognize Queen material, and you can take comfort in your blue ribbons. Or send a snapshot to me; I'll be very proud of you.

And if you find a way to grow Color Magic without dieback, *please* let me know.

Acknowledgments

My thanks to Robert Galyean, the foreman at Garden Valley Ranch, for mastering every technique in this book—and improving on some—to grow roses worth writing about; William Derveniotes for grooming those blooms that weren't quite perfect and for being my consulting rosarian; Adair Lara for teaching me how to write this book and for showing me how to move my words around until they make sense; M. F. K. Fisher for giving me goose bumps when she said she'd write a foreword for me, and again every time I reread it; and many friends, especially members of the staff and board of directors of the San Francisco Hearing & Speech Center, for knowing that roses compose my second wonderful world.

RCR

Index